THE KIDSPACE
IDEA BOOK

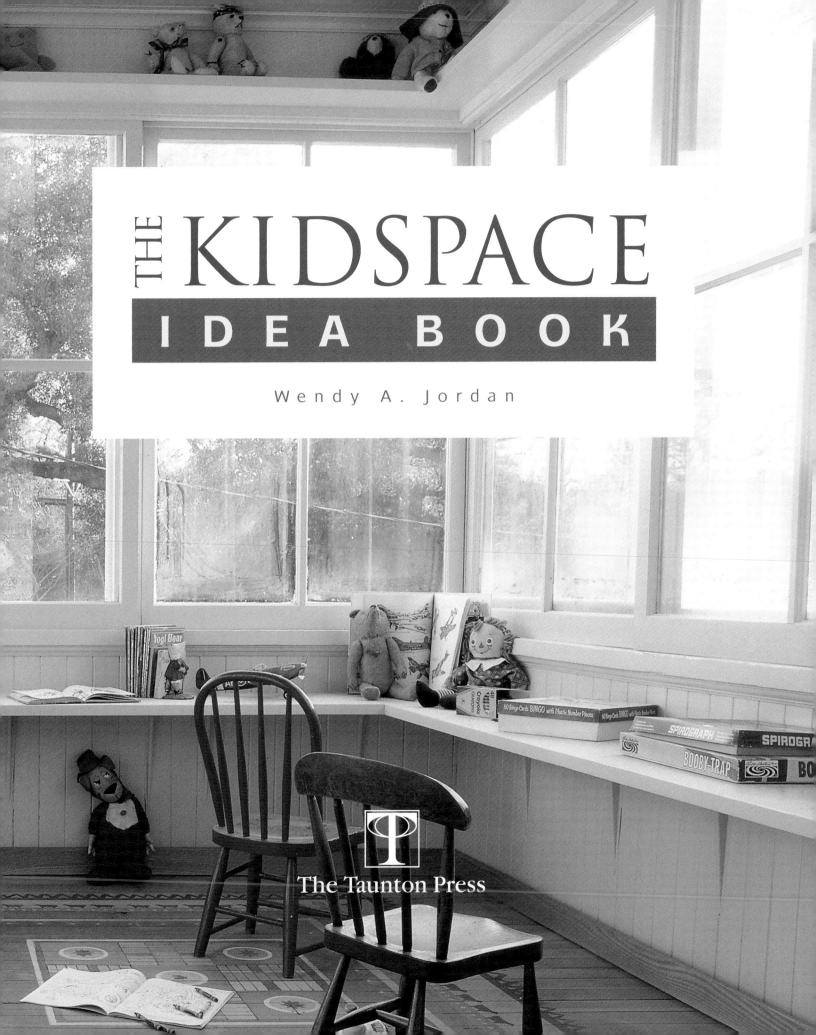

THE KIDSPACE
IDEA BOOK

Wendy A. Jordan

The Taunton Press

To Heather

PUBLISHER
Jim Childs

ACQUISITIONS EDITOR
Steve Culpepper

EDITORIAL ASSISTANT
Carol Kasper

COPY EDITOR
Candace B. Levy

DESIGNER
Carol Singer

LAYOUT ARTIST
Cathy Cassidy

ILLUSTRATOR
Christine Erikson

BOOKS & VIDEOS

for fellow enthusiasts

Printed in Singapore
10 9 8 7 6 5 4 3 2 1

The Taunton Press, Inc., 63 South Main Street, PO Box 5506, Newtown, CT 06470-5506
e-mail: tp@taunton.com

Distributed by Publishers Group West

Library of Congress Cataloging-in Publication Data:

Jordan, Wendy Adler, 1946-
      The kidspace idea book / Wendy A. Jordan.
          p. cm.
      ISBN 1-56158-352-9
      1. Children's rooms—Planning. 2. Interior decoration—Human factors. I. Title.
NK2117.C4 J67 2001
747.7—dc21   00-051026

Acknowledgments

This book is a lot like one of those human pyramids formed by gymnasts. In the gymnastics performance, experienced pros take the bottom row, establishing a strong, stable base. Additional talented athletes balance on the shoulders of those pros, displaying their own elan. At the peak of the pyramid, more often than not, is a child—beaming with excitement and pride.

Many knowledgeable, creative people helped build this book. At the base of the pyramid is an understanding of kids and the kinds of spaces that are best for them. I'm grateful to all the experts who helped build that foundation, including Stevanne Auerbach, Ph.D., Institute of Childhood Resources, San Francisco; Dana Blackwell, Kidfacts Research, Troy, Michigan; Susan Goltsman, MIG, Inc., and PLAE, Inc., Berkeley, California; Sandra Hofferth, University of Michigan Institute for Social Research, Ann Arbor; Ann Howard, Ph.D., clinical psychologist, Chevy Chase, Maryland; Patrick Manning, Ergonomic Solutions, Cleveland; Dale Mulfinger, AIA, SALA Architects, Minneapolis; John P. Robinson, Ph.D., University of Maryland, College Park; Rita Schonberg, Ph.D., clinical psychologist, Chevy Chase, Maryland.; Sarah Susanka, AIA, Minneapolis; and Louis Torelli, Spaces for Children, Berkeley, California.

Scores of architects, designers, ingenious homeowners, and others fill the next tiers of the pyramid. These gifted people gave shape to the book by generously sharing their ideas and inspirations for kids' spaces. My thanks go to them all. A great many are credited in the back, because their projects appear in the book. Others include Alice Busch, ASID, Great Falls Distinctive Interiors, Great Falls, Virginia; Linda Kay DeMartini, ASID, Kay Designs, Burlingame, California; Lynne Enerson, Cottage Grove, Wisconsin; Phyllis Goldberg, ASID, PPG Interiors, Providence, Rhode Island; John Hermannsson, AIA, Redwood City, California; Sarah Boyer Jenkins, FASID, Sarah Boyer Jenkins and Associates, Chevy Chase, Maryland; Bruce Johnson, AIA, Asheville, North Carolina; Jim Krengel, CKD, CBD, Kitchens by Krengel, St. Paul; Marcello Luzi, ASID, Weixler, Peterson and Luzi, Philadelphia; Irene Paige, Washington, D.C.; Mary Jo Peterson, CKD, CBD, Mary Jo Peterson, Inc., Brookfield, Connecticut; Barbara Schlattman, ASID, Barbara Schlattman Interiors, Houston; Rick Share, Rick Share Architect, New York; Alene Workman, ASID, Alene Workman Interior Design, Hollywood, Florida; and Joni Zimmerman, CKD, CBD, Design Solutions, Annapolis, Maryland. Thanks also to the California Peninsula Chapter ASID, Menlo Park, California; Community Playthings, Elka Park, New York; and the Museum of Contemporary Art, Chicago. If I have omitted any names, it is inadvertent and I apologize.

Acquisitions Editor Steve Culpepper at The Taunton Press pushed the book to new heights. I admire his talent and vision. Likewise, I thank all the other Taunton staff who contributed their time and skills, especially Carol Kasper, Carolyn Mandarano, Wendi Mijal, Jennifer Renjilian, and Art Director Paula Schlosser.

Thanks to Karen Barr for helping to scout projects, to the many photographers around the country who captured great kids' spaces on camera, and above all to the families who welcomed us into their homes so that we could photograph their kids' spaces and share them with readers.

At the top of the pyramid? Kids, of course. They are the spark behind the joyful designs collected in this book. Here's to them all.

Contents

Introduction ▪ 3

Chapter 1
Houses Made
for Children ▪ 4

So What Are the Trends? ▪ **6**

Planning for What You Want ▪ **11**

Great Family Areas ▪ **14**

Look for Overlooked Space ▪ **17**

The Great Backyard ▪ **21**

About This Book ▪ **23**

Chapter 2
Bedrooms
and Baths ▪ 24

Beginning with the Nursery ▪ **28**

Rooms for Toddlers ▪ **32**

Rooms for Grade Schoolers ▪ **38**

Almost Teenagers ▪ **54**

The Teenager's Room ▪ **62**

Bathrooms for Kids ▪ **70**

A Place for Everything ▪ **78**

Chapter 3
Places Built Just for Kids • 86

Suites • **88**

Playrooms • **94**

Hideaways • **104**

Places to Do Homework • **112**

Special-Activity Rooms • **117**

Chapter 4
Rooms for the Whole Family • 122

Family Rooms • **126**

Kitchens and Eating Areas • **133**

Stowing Gear • **140**

Chapter 5
Playing Outside • 146

Basic Play Areas • **148**

Playhouses • **152**

Tree Houses • **160**

Resources • 168

Credits • 169

Gentle curves in the woodwork make these
built-in bunkbeds as beautiful as they are fun
to use. And tucked behind the paneling are
private shelves and cubbies for each child.

The American family has outgrown American home design. As family lifestyles have changed, philosophies of home design haven't kept up. Fairyland children's bedrooms, for example, may still delight the parents, but these static stage sets bore the kids, cramp their creativity, and get old—fast. Even more neglected are all those areas of the house that are used not by the kids alone but by the entire family. In most homes today, there are two ways to use the kitchen, living area, deck, and other family spaces—the adult way or the wrong way.

Like a much-needed new pair of shoes for a kid who's outgrown the old ones, The *Kidspace Idea Book* fits the American family comfortably and well. It's filled with good, fresh, practical design ideas to mold family spaces to the way they function for both kids and adults in the house. It tells how to design kids' spaces that work—really work—for the kids.

Through photos and plans, each section of the book covers a different area of the house and then moves outside, from bedroom to playroom, kitchen to tree house. Detail photos zoom in on design ideas that help make a good room better. Features sprinkled throughout the book highlight special-interest topics, such as shared bedrooms, small rooms, suites, rooms for twins, and hobby areas. Quick-read sidebars cover safety, colors, lighting, and other essentials.

This is a practical, pointed, and friendly book. Use it as a launching point for the design of great family and kid spaces.

Houses Made for Children

Admit it. When we were growing up, most places for kids in and around the home were boring. Living areas were not particularly welcoming for kids. Bedrooms and baths were boxy and uninspired. Playhouses were generic. Even most tree houses lacked flair. But family lifestyles are less formal now, more go-with-the-flow—and so are our houses.

Bedrooms and bathrooms for children have undergone a transformation from something strictly utilitarian to something that not only works well but looks good. And the rest of the house is catching up, with family rooms, playrooms, and living rooms all designed and constructed with kids in mind.

We've come a long way from the children-should-be-seen-and-not-heard days. Now, happily, our lives center around our kids, and we want our houses to reflect that commitment. We want living areas that welcome the whole family, and kids' rooms that are nurturing environments in which our children play, learn, and grow.

What a pleasant change. Now the whole house sends kids a message that says: "This is your home, too."

We relax in family rooms, great rooms, and media rooms that are designed for peaceful coexistence of adults and kids. Even our living rooms are going casual. There's a place for the whole crowd to gather around the television to

◄Kids on both sides of these open, adjustable shelves share sunlight and access to the books—but enjoy a little privacy too. A library ladder on a horseshoe track puts high shelves within reach. For a breath of fresh air, the kids can step out on the balcony.

watch a movie, plus an intimate corner for conversation or for a quiet interlude with a good book. The kids are welcome to play on the floor or pull up a chair in front of the computer.

And spaces built just for kids include lofts, suites, playhouses, secret hide-aways, built-in aquariums, indoor basketball hoops, stages, walls of colorful storage, high-tech homework centers, and splashy bathrooms. Outside, there are cool forts and tree houses, clubhouses and playhouses that let kids make their own adventure.

So What Are the Trends?

The best designs I've run across do a number of things well. First on the list is that "yes" you feel when entering a

▲The playhouse on stilts is small enough to fit little children but roomy enough to hold three sleeping bags for overnights. Safe, operable windows capture breezes, and a skylight soaks in the sun. The playhouse forms a roof over the sandbox. With its white columns, fine woods, and craftsman details, its also a landscape asset.

▶Built-ins make this room useful and interesting. A built-in desk offers tree-house views from the second floor of this timber-frame home. Drawers beneath the built-in bed make use of an often overlooked storage area.

◀This structure turns one play area into three: an airy loft, a cozy under-loft alcove, and an open playroom with reading corner. Deep and tall, the storage cubbies are versatile. The loft railings combine function and fantasy.

home that was thoughtfully designed with children in mind. The very best kids' spaces in this book were designed so that kids can run around with friends or play alone, explore new interests, display things they like, engage in make-believe, and make a mess—all without being told, "No, not here."

They're Where They Should Be

The younger the child, the closer to you he or she wants to be. Toddlers like to be right in the room with you—especially, it seems, in the kitchen. The best family kitchen designs take into account the fact that helpers will be close at hand. These little ones obviously can't be with

◀A fold-down stool mounted inside a cabinet door brings the microwave or sink within kids' reach. Stools like this are available from numerous manufacturers.

you around the clock, however, so their bedrooms belong within earshot. Five-year-olds are okay playing alone if you're not too far away; they don't need to be in the same room but close enough that they can hear or see you. By age eight or so, kids move farther afield, to the attic playroom or basement den.

Grab All the Space You Can

Take a look at the playroom in chapter 3 (p. 101) that was created from unused attic space in a bungalow remodel. The playroom is open to the stairwell so parents can be alert to any problems. On p. 114, you'll see, a study hall created in a large second-floor landing of a ranch house remodel that's also open to the stairwell—but this time it's so the parents can keep watch on what their teenagers are getting into online.

The best kids' spaces also are organized, at least loosely, into areas. Kids are much happier if the space is cut into small zones set up for different activities—arts and crafts here, dress-up there, a book nook in the corner.

Make your kids' spaces low maintenance too. Go with wipe-clean laminates

Flooring for Families

The rooms shown throughout this book look great and work well. But underneath everything is the flooring, which often goes overlooked as a functioning part of a kid's space. Flooring certainly should be part of the planning process for any kid's space.

Flooring suitable for family areas is durable and easy care, but that doesn't mean it needs to be a step down in style. Some of the best-looking flooring is also practical and hard wearing.

In chapter 4, notice that the kitchens and other uncarpeted spaces where kids play with wheeled toys, build castles, and do art projects often are covered with flooring that's smooth and waterproof, such as ceramic tile or wood that's coated with a waterproof seal. And for family areas, kids bedrooms, and playrooms, low-pile, dense-weave carpeting seems to be the best choice because it wears well and hides dirt.

◀▼In this home kitchen of a professional chef, the center island is naturally at the heart of family activities. Easy-access basket-drawers hold both vegetables and kids' art supplies, which is a creative way to both welcome children to the kitchen and accommodate their needs.

▲Instead of segregating the bedrooms of their two young daughters and giving each a separate closet of her own, the parents got innovative. The girls share one walk-through closet that's full of built-ins and clothes storage. It also lets them visit privately, rather than shutting themselves off.

and waterproof flooring so kids can do their thing with abandon. The kids'll be happier and so will parents. Yet while these are carefree places, they also need to be safe. It goes without saying that rooms for kids are accident proof.

Using Innovation and Inspiration

The kids' spaces shown in this book have cabinets, shelves, baskets, bins, and closets enough to hold it all. And things are stored near where kids are likely to use them, making it that much more likely the kids will put things away when they're done. Theoretically.

Parents have gotten fanciful with space, creating worlds of fantasy that match their kids' interests and perhaps fulfill some dreams of their own. Or else they've found some little bit of unused space—between rooms, overhead, down below, out back—and turned them into a tiny, interesting place that kids really love.

Kids love rooms with structure, shape, and the promise of adventure. They can't resist ladders to climb, overhangs to crawl under, lofts to perch atop, cozy hollows to curl up inside of, cutouts to peek through. Look at the tree houses in chapter 5. Or the castle within a room in chapter 2. Or the hideaway in the wall of a teenager's bedroom in chapter 3.

Kids' Spaces Are the Right Size

When kids are small, their rooms reach down to meet them, so to speak. Not everything in the room should be small, though. Kids outgrow overly kid-scaled rooms in a flash.

Remember forts made with blankets and chairs? Well, the new kids' spaces go a giant step better. Imagine the magic of

▶Planning requires creative thinking, which explains this kids' playroom, built atop the garage. The room is acoustically separate from the main house, so kids can play loud music, cut up, and make a mess without disrupting the main living spaces in the home.

a built-in cove or a lookout loft—or a whole secret room reached via a door camouflaged as a bookcase. And the truth is, kids never outgrow the lure of secret places. The hideaway behind a false front in chapter 3 (see p. 109) is the prized sanctuary of a teenager.

Of all these trends, the most important is this: These rooms can grow and change as the kids grow and change. Moveable modules and adjustable shelves let kids reinvent their rooms when the mood strikes. But some rooms contain such clever built-ins that all they need is a new coat of paint and up-to-date accessories to make the transition from little kid's room to teenager's room.

Planning for What You Want

Parents can design their own places for kids. But getting help from an architect, builder, remodeler, kitchen and bath specialist, or interior designer can be the quickest and most efficient way to get started. Often these residential design pros work as a team, one concentrating on the overall plan and the sticks and bricks of construction while the other handles the details.

Many professionals will help homeowners on a consulting basis to evaluate the feasibility of remodeling a house, design new or remodeled space, or draw

Giving Kids Some Space

A Texas couple with four children realized that both parents and children needed some space of their own. The result is a central family area flanked by the master suite at one end and a kids' wing at the other. The older children got their own bedrooms and the two younger ones shared a bedroom, all of which connect to a large playroom. The children also got a loft over the dining room that overlooks the living room and kitchen, and a large, covered outdoor play pavilion.

▲Although the kids in this house command a wing featuring bedrooms, baths, and playroom, they still spend some time during the day in their parents' room watching the television, which slides out of sight and hides behind a closed door.

A Children's Suite

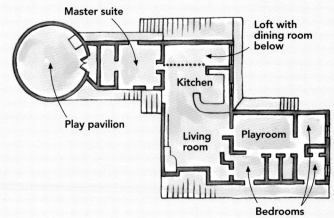

▲Punched through a low wall, this small niche is packed with play power. With deeply pitched ceiling, central corner, and mosaic window walls, it works equally as sunny outpost or cozy getaway.

up engineering plans. It's especially handy to have an architect prepare working drawings and shepherd the project through the permits and approvals process.

Seeking Some Professional Help

Hiring an architect or design professional is usually money well spent. A few hours of an achitect's time provides years of experience and firsthand, up-to-date knowledge of what works and what doesn't. These pros are familiar with important considerations, such as traffic flow and sound insulation in and between rooms; ventilation; door clearances; the size addition that's allowed in a particular neighborhood; and code requirements for stairs, window sizes and locations, and other factors that might come into play.

They'll also be able to tell which walls are load bearing and can't be removed, where the plumbing stacks and pipes are (meaning where it's most practical to add a bathroom or sink), and whether the electrical system needs upgrading. These professionals might offer solutions to vexing problems, such as how to fit a door into a tight corner (install a pocket door) or squeeze more storage into a small bathroom (one idea: slip in some shelves between the wall studs). And they'll have information on products and materials and costs.

Getting Started on Your Own

Most parents are capable of designing and building great kids' spaces on their own. The ideas in this book provide a head start. As for the construction, homeowners should familiarize themselves with applicable building requirements, bone up on construction techniques, and then start planning.

Study how the house is used. Make a list of things that need to be changed to accommodate the family, enliven the kids' rooms, and manage the clutter wherever it accumulates. Obviously, working within the existing walls is simplest, but a bump-out or one-story addition need not be overly complicated.

Looking through a Child's Eyes

The best way to design kids' spaces is to try to think as a kid thinks. Watch kids in action to get ideas, too. What are their favorite activities? Play up those activities when planning the space. It's also smart to include an inviting place that encourages kids to do things they should do

Hiring an Architect

If you believe you need an architect to help you design your new house or to remodel your existing house—but are afraid of the cost commitment of hiring one—here are some things the American Institute of Architects suggests you consider.

First, there is no set fee. A few options for architectural services include paying on an hourly basis, agreeing on a fee up front based on the plan the architect proposes, paying the architect based on the square footage of the house or remodel, and a combination of these.

Surveys show that an architects' fees range from 5 to 15 percent of the cost of the new house or remodel, though the location of the house (local cost of living), the level of detail in the house, and the size of the project are all factors.

Whatever amount homeowners pay, the fee should reflect their confidence in the architect. And in all cases, whether using an architect, a designer, or a designer/builder, get everything in writing. Contracts are an essential part of any construction project and include a standard agreement between owner and contractor, a standard agreement between owner and architect, change orders (when building conditions or the owners require changes in the design during construction), an application and certificate for payment, and a certificate of substantial completion.

▲Large, open family areas are a significant trend in new and remodeled homes. These loosely structured spaces make room for the whole family, with areas for cooking, eating, reading, and just sitting and talking.

▲The low ceiling makes this attic room just right for a young child. Roof windows admit light and air without causing safety concerns. Bright wallpaper turns the low wall into a design highlight.

▶For smaller children, a play area that's close to parents gives a sense of comfort and connectedness. Using the imagination of a child, the architect-father of these children created a wide landing at the top of the stairs as a play space for his kids.

more, such as reading or drawing. And every kid needs a retreat where he or she can go for quiet time alone. A sheltered corner, or even a bed alcove, can be that private haven.

Kids have creative design ideas of their own. Even the youngest kids have particular preferences if offered a choice. They want a blue room, or a wall they can write on, or an area to play house. They may figure out ways to do things you never imagined.

Great Family Areas

The best family areas are well-lit, open spaces with subtly defined zones that let everyone feel connected. If your house is like mine—a warren of small rooms— there's a lot you can do to open it up. A nearly cost-free way to create a more open flow among kitchen, dining room, living room, and den is simply to remove a door or two.

In some homes, it's possible to remove a wall to get a great room or family room that's large enough for media corner, play space, and a spot for snacks. A more daring approach is to open the space upward. A family that bought an old house with a dark, boxy, formal living room took out the living room ceiling (and the bedroom above it) to gain a two-story space and a broad, second-floor loft overlooking the living area.

Reinventing Unused Rooms

Except when polished up for Thanksgiving and Christmas, our dining room was little more than a repository for mail. We always ate at the family room table or the kitchen counter, because it was casual and convenient. But with TV, phone, and stereo, my family room had *too much* going on. So I "threw out" the dining room and reconfigured it as a comfortable study, outfitted with bookshelves, desk, and overstuffed chairs. Now we have a network of family spaces after removing the doors that separated them.

Even closets and other storage areas are prime candidates for new uses. Turn a broom closet into a kitchen computer center. Pull out a base cabinet to make way for a kids' desk or kitchen play station. Convert the closet by the back door into a mudroom, with bench, hooks, cubbies, and shelves.

Older homes tend to be laced with hallways that waste space. Give some of that space to adjacent rooms to make bigger, more versatile living areas. Or add a blackboard or toy cabinet to make a little play area in the hallway right around the corner from the kitchen. Architect Sarah Susanka designed a house with a loop of hallways in the living area. It's just the place for kids to race around and burn off energy (see p. 129).

▲The kids are out of the kitchen but not out of sight when they play in this family room. The pass-through counter spaces are windows into the corner where the kids' toys are stowed.

Capitalizing on Wasted Space

Lofts or playrooms carved from what otherwise would be unused attic space are extremely popular now and for good reason: kids love them. Wherever there's dead attic space or wherever a ceiling next to a child's bedroom can be lowered (like over the closets, as shown below right), there's room for a little hideaway loft. Access by ladder makes it even more of an adventure. Larger attic space can be used for media rooms, homework rooms, or playrooms, as in the photo below.

Room above the Closets

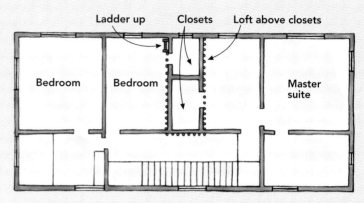

Ladder up   Closets   Loft above closets

Bedroom   Bedroom   Master suite

▲This room was planned as attic storage before the parents and the architect realized that it would make a great place for kids to play. It gets a bit of natural light from the small window, and the colors also help brighten it up.

▶A small child's room seems much bigger than it is thanks to careful use of molding, clever paint combinations (the white above the molding and on the ceiling seems to add height to the room), and the little loft above the closet.

◀This two-story-high gym, with its whimsical serpentine and spiral paths, is set up for active play. Lighting is inset, surfaces are rugged, roomy toy garages store tricycles and sports equipment. Overlooking the gym is a more intimate upstairs room for games and other sedate play.

Look for Overlooked Space

While scouting for kids-only spaces around the house, look for unconventional spaces. Children love them. Odd corners, overhangs, and nooks and crannies that seem of little practical use may be just the place for private, kids-size clubhouses or retreats. Look under the stairs, beneath the low ceiling in the far reaches of the attic playroom, in window recesses. Almost no space is too small to appeal to kids. And the more private and self-contained the better. When her house

was being remodeled, architect Steven Foote's young daughter claimed a perch above the stairs. Captivated by her idea, Foote gave the perch a porthole window, camouflaged steps, and a secret door worthy of Harry Potter himself (see p. 104).

Start thinking like Foote and even closets can become imagination stations. Take off the closet door to make a playhouse. Add a curtain to create a theater. Turn the top shelf into a loft. Convert the closet into a compact study center. The roomy closet in the 14-year-old boy's room shown on p. 68 became a one-of-

► It doesn't take a lot to give a child's room special appeal. A full-height mirror between two windows adds a sense of depth to this girl's room. And the dancing barre attached over the mirror lets the girl enjoy one of her passions. Storage here is simple and out in the open with the stacked plastic bins.

a-kind bed cabinet. As his father, architect D'Arcy Dunal, said, "Teenagers never hang anything up in the closet anyway, so why not turn the space into something more interesting?"

If a house lacks quirky spaces in the right places it's no problem. Just build interest into kids' rooms. Younger kids make resourceful, creative use of step-up play areas. They love colorful bed platforms with toy storage underneath. Kids any age go for lofts. A simple project that gets rave reviews from kids is a bed enclosure. I've collected examples of each. Just craft a deep overhang, install a couple of sheltering panels made of wood or fabric, and put a bookshelf and reading light inside: The bed becomes a retreat.

See Stuff through a Child's Eyes

Like adults, kids feel more comfortable when things around them are neat and orderly. There are a couple of key things to keep in mind when helping children organize their possessions. First, see to it that they have a place for everything. If each type of toy has a "home," they won't have an excuse for leaving it on the floor. Second, label all the bins and baskets so the message is even clearer. And when organizing a kids' room, start at the bottom, where they are, and work your way up, with the most-used things nearest the floor.

Seek Out Small Innovations

Creative dividers make kids' rooms, even fairly small ones, more interesting and more functional because they organize the space. Gone is the box. In its place is a magical and inviting place. In a room for one child, use a partition to split the space into bedroom and play area; a counter on the playroom side of the partition adds a work surface for art projects.

◀At the top of the open stairs in this Washington state home is a big open room that's used by all the kids in the family for homework, art projects, and playing. Because the room takes up the entire top level of the house, the kids do what they want without being underfoot.

▼Before the space was remodeled, two preteens used to share a bath and have ladder access to small attic rooms. Now they share the attic but have separate baths. The trade was a great deal. Bumped out a few feet, the remodeled suite gives each girl a larger bedroom and her own stairs to a dramatic, skylighted loft that's big enough for the sisters and their friends to get together.

If kids have their own adjoining rooms, they probably wouldn't mind linking up some of the time. Interior window cutouts, tunnels, and shared lofts soften the barrier between rooms and give kids a shared adventure.

Paint Alone Can Create Change

Even innovative finishes may be enough to transform your kids' rooms into playful spaces. Tile the floor to make a game board or curlicue path or patchwork of bold-colored activity zones. If you've got the space in the basement, paint a hockey rink or basketball court. For a hands-on room, cover a wall or countertop with chalkboard paint or a wipe-off art surface. Another option is to cover a wall with magnetic or corkboard panels. In the kids' bathroom, scatter a few

whimsical tiles across the wall, maybe even custom tiles showing the family dog or your kids' art. And how about a smooth tile panel by the bathtub, where kids can create pictures with bathtub "fingerpaint"?

▶It's not beautiful, but it works. This patchwork tree house has everything a kid could want—slide, rope swing, balcony, trapdoor.

Making Connections

A hot trend in new homes is kids' suites or interconnected rooms that meet children's every need. A suite for one child is almost like an apartment. It includes a bedroom, play area, and study space in an open plan, plus its own bathroom. As you'll see later in the book, suites for several kids place the bedrooms like spokes around a central study or play area. Some of the suites for teens even

have snack kitchens and direct outdoor access. A modified version is a shared study center, with bookshelves, computer, and tables and chairs. In some houses it's a whole room; in others, it's bonus space on a broad landing. Suites give kids their own realm under your roof. Just don't make them too removed from the center of family activity, or the kids will become strangers.

The Great Backyard

"Go outside and play" used to be what parents told kids who were in the way. Today it's an invitation to enjoy a backyard adventure. The latest outdoor play structures are splendid. They're imaginative, versatile, and brimming with play options for one kid or a crowd. And that's a good thing, because one thing hasn't changed: He who has the best backyard play equipment ends up with all the neighborhood kids in his yard.

Backyard playhouses range from the very basic to the elaborate. In this book you'll see some that are vividly colorful fantasy buildings complete with upstairs and downstairs levels, "furnished" kitchens, windows, lighting, mail slots, porches, and landscaping. And some tree houses are just as elaborate, with lofts and towers and quick-exit routes via rope or rippling slide. Ho-hum swing sets have been replaced by play centers that stretch across the yard, linking a variety of goodies, from swings and bridges to lookout posts.

Create Action and Adventure

These outdoor structures aren't necessarily just for kids; some tree houses and swings are big enough for Mom and Dad to seize the moment and climb aboard.

An increasing number of architects and artisans specialize in designing and creating outdoor play structures. They design everything from charming little playhouses to deluxe creations, custom tailored to coordinate with the house on the property. And, sure, you can buy kits and plans for playhouses and play sets. But why do that when some of the best backyard play structures are homemade?

Pick a theme that delights your kids and build on it. Forts and cozy little gingerbread houses are ever popular. More exotic themes—castles and ships and rockets and circus wagons—also make great play zones.

Outdoor play spaces needn't be big on size as long as they're big on interest.

▲Could it get any better than this? A twin-tower-covered play set satisfies all basic kid requirements: chute-slide, ladder, swings, stairs, lookouts, and a sandbox.

▼This post-mounted lodge has the trappings of a tree house, including rope ladder, trapdoor, and hook-and-pulley for hoisting supplies. A rear wall gives a sense of enclosure, but parents can keep an eye on things from the front—or, as they've often done, climb up for a family picnic. The pressure-treated lumber and cedar shingles will age gracefully.

▲Although rain's usually not a problem in this arid part of Texas, this large round play pavilion certainly gives these kids a break from the intense Austin summer sun. The concrete floor is also the cover for the family's cistern.

Watch kids in action at the playground or museum; their favorite places are the ones they can get into or on top of and the ones with moving parts like steering wheels and telephone receivers and swaying bridges and little doors. Things to do and things that move: They are also the hot buttons for backyard play structures.

Don't Overlook Hills and Dales

Some of the most unlikely places make the best spots for play structures, because they invite fun, one-of-a-kind designs. Does the yard slope steeply? Just the place for a playhouse on stilts, with two stories hugging the hillside and a slide out the side door. Create a clubhouse on top of a storage shed or detached garage, or attach it to an outside wall. Clusters of trees offer the makings of a multitree tree house, with bridges from trunk to trunk. Small yard? Check out the double-decker design above left, where a playhouse perches on piers right over the sandbox.

The best family spaces outside are seg-mented into a variety of areas so every-one can spread out and enjoy the fresh air while doing different things. Decks, patios, and porches bend around corners and step up and down to form separate spaces for grilling hamburgers, swinging in a hammock, and enjoying the sun.

About This Book

This book is easy to use because it's arranged by area of the house. Chapter 2 highlights bedrooms for different age groups, from infants to teens, as well as bathrooms and storage areas. Chapter 3 covers playrooms, studies, and a new kind of space that's getting a lot of attention these days—hideaways. Chapter 5 is filled with ideas for those wondrous new out-door structures that are turning backyards into play heaven.

And this book breaks new ground by featuring ideas for kids' spaces all around the home. Because family areas now are being designed to incorporate kids' activi-ties, I've included family rooms, kid-friendly kitchens, and gear zones.

The photos and plans in the book showcase the best ideas for kid's spaces. In the text, sidebars, and captions, I ex-plain why the ideas work well and offer tips on how to implement them.

A list of useful resources appears in the back of the book, as do credits for the projects shown.

▲ A kid's bathroom doesn't have to look like an ordinary bathroom—in fact, the wilder, the better. The children's bathroom in this seaside house borrows from beach themes of cabanas and strings of lights.

The creative tools are here—the ideas, the examples, and the practical guide-lines. To produce great spaces for your kids, just put those tools to work.

Bedrooms and Baths

▶Sponge-painted tiles, made by the family's toddlers on an outing to the local paint-your-own-pottery store, make this bathroom shine. Once the tiles were fired, the homeowners laid them out on the floor to plan the wall montage.

Whoever the child, whatever the age, successful kids' spaces are places where children are comfortable and where they enjoy spending time playing, working, or hanging out. Through all the ages of childhood and all the variations of bedrooms and baths, these basics never change. Yet opportunities to make improvements are always available to parents, whether planning a simple makeover, a complete remodel, an addition, or even a new house.

Without a doubt, two of the most important rooms for children are the bedroom and the bathroom. The best of these rooms are functional, organized, versatile, and, above all,

◀The fun and adventure rise in this room, from the bunk bed to the wall-climbing ladder to the loft, which is fitted out like a tiny room in itself.

adaptable. So as kids grow and change, these rooms can be reinvented without a lot of hassle and expense—if the process begins with good planning. Throughout this chapter, I show a number of different bedrooms and bathrooms, each planned and designed for children of a particular age, yet all able to stay in tune with growing children.

The first step in the planning process is understanding what you want to accomplish. What is the goal of a remodel or new construction? The answer helps establish priorities— what's most important and what are merely wishes (this part of the process works best if the whole family gets involved). Eventually, the list gets fairly long; but as it develops, priorities get sorted so that at the top are the necessities (bigger closet, new bathroom, better lighting), and at the bottom are the pipe dreams (indoor basketball court, 1,000-gallon aquarium, candy machine). Needless to say, the line usually gets drawn somewhere near the top of the list.

Designing the space takes a different kind of discipline. And though an experienced architect is worth his or her weight in gold, homeowners usually get the best results if they

◄Simple cubes become a witty design component when finished with colorful laminate or paint and stepped up the wall. Red pulls and a belt of blue spice up these basic drawers, too.

▼A swath of fabric and a simple dowel hung from the ceiling turn this bed area into a tranquil retreat sheltered from the window. With custom slots for sound system, VCR, and television, the wall unit keeps bulky high-tech gear from dominating the room.

do their homework. The trick is to take a long, hard look at other kids' spaces. This includes starting a clipping file and reviewing magazines and books. Just remember the basic rule: The room should be a comfortable place where kids enjoy spending time. One classic design trick is to create one or two centers of interest in the room. This might be a loft, a bed structure with cabinets, a built-in aquarium, a window seat, or a reading nook.

Even a quirky room can present fresh opportunities. A narrow wall might be just the place for a magazine or coloring-book rack. A sliding panel can transform under-cabinet kick space into "secret" storage. Nest an upholstered seat or desk into a dormer window niche.

In small rooms, such as a child's bathroom, a little personal style goes a long way, so it's best to stick to a few featured highlights the kids will enjoy, which also will make it easier to revise the room as the kids grow older. Although you need not limit your options to off-the-shelf parts, manufacturers of bath fixtures and fittings, tile, lighting fixtures, modular furniture systems, flooring, beds, desks, and cabinetry all have products specifically designed for kids. ✳

Beginning with the Nursery

A key point for parents to remember is that a nursery should work both for parents and the baby. Although it is the baby's room, the parents will spend a lot of time there. Another thing to keep in mind is that babies don't stay little for long. As anybody with a teenager can attest, children grow up fast; so the room that looked precious and perfect for your infant quickly looks outdated for a toddler.

However, most of what changes in a kid's room between babyhood and college can be superficial: furniture, drapes, paint, posters. But if a remodel, addition, or new home is planned, consider certain eventualities: Will there be more children? Can they share a bedroom? Is the nursery big enough to serve eventually as a teenager's room or will the child need to move to a bigger room? Will the house need another bathroom or will an adjoining bathroom be required?

Also remember that if the nursery isn't going to be the child's permanent bedroom—say it'll eventually be a playroom, library, home office, or guest room—do some

▲Perimeter shelves, a wallpaper border, and soft white walls prove that, even in a volume space, you can craft a cozy area for the baby. Clouds and a balloon floating aloft act as overhead scenery. To filter light from the odd-shaped window, the homeowners installed operable custom shutters.

►This room was a study until the baby came along, yet the room's low soffit creates an intimate space for a nursery area. Here the crib nestles into a star-spangled niche formed by the deep soffit and twin bookcases.

▼A ribbon of narrow shelving just below the ceiling turns small toys and curios into a wraparound "picture" in the baby's room. Easy to assemble using prefabricated trim, such shelving visually lowers the height of the room, making it more intimate.

Changing Tables

In a small room, an old dresser converts nicely into a changing table, with drawers below and a soft pad with safety straps on top. Take advantage of wall space, too, to make the small room more flexible. Consider encircling the room with high shelves, which will hold toys now and display trophies and collections when the child is older.

◀Even frilly white appointments can be practical and hardworking. The pretty framed shelves, for instance, can hold supplies as well as collectibles. Wraparound wall treatments—in this case painted sashes—tie together an odd-shaped space.

▲You can use grown-up elements in a baby's room. The vintage wall shelf and changing table harmonize with the classic architecture of this room. And, although the shelf is dressed down here with nursery things, when the baby grows up she can toss clothes onto those hooks. Maybe the changing table will hold her CD player.

advance planning for wiring, built-ins, and other storage so the room will be ready for other uses when the time comes.

Certain improvements can prove valuable for all ages. If you are building or remodeling, a wired-in intercom system is a good investment. The intercom lets parents mind the baby and, later, call the older kids to dinner. And for teenagers, an intercom may be one of the few ways parents have of direct communication. Wireless models are also available for existing homes.

As far as the room goes, any well-ventilated space will work as a baby's room. And for as long as it will be a baby's room, imagination can help make it work better. ✳

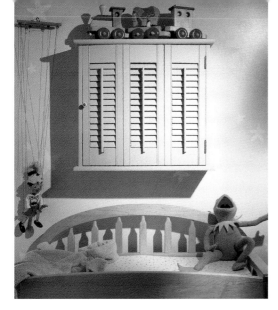

◄Keep supplies handy but out of sight in a shuttered cabinet over the changing table. Repaint the cabinet, remount it, or remove its doors when the baby gets older.

Mechanical Considerations

Mechanical and electrical systems are often overlooked but are important—especially for a nursery. Whatever and wherever the room, it should maintain a comfortable, consistent temperature and be well ventilated but draft free. For lighting, soft overhead lighting, task lighting, and a night-light will do the job right now. If constructing the baby's room from scratch, plan ahead by installing plenty of outlets, along with wiring for a computer and phone, not important now but necessities later.

▼A few bold, well-chosen color accents make this room cheerful and fun. Highlights include the painted faux balloons and the dresser that's been pepped up by a clever paint job. To tame the oversize window, the designer used a dimensional valance that narrows to a point at the center of the "big top."

Rooms for Toddlers

Toddlers are like electric lights: on or off. When they're on, they're climbing, rolling, reaching, and exploring, so their rooms—and the whole house—should be organized accordingly. But when it's time for lights out, kids this age need to recharge in a quiet, comfortable, and uncluttered spot in their rooms.

As the room gets put together, bring everything down to kids'-eye level for the time being. That means low shelves that toddlers can reach easily without climbing (shelves and cabinets absolutely must be secured to the wall). It means low platforms and surfaces toddlers can climb up or sit on. It means low drawers, cabinets, closet rods, and big hooks that toddlers can use without help. (At this age, doing something by themselves—including hanging up their pajamas—is an achievement.) It means hanging not only blackboards and mirrors but also pictures low on

▲ This neat room may stay that way because the storage cubes and baskets are low, large, and easy for toddlers to reach from the play table. The built-in toy box under the window works equally well as seat or tabletop.

the walls. If the room's being constructed, it means installing windows low enough that the kids can see out. And, of course, it means that second-floor windows should have protective coverings.

Apart from storage and furniture, the rest of the room is a matter of taste. Most parents try to develop a theme for their toddler's room. A zoo, a storybook world, a train. Whatever the theme, two conditions should be met: The theme should appeal strongly to the child, and it should be applied in moderation, so there's room for the child's imagination to follow other paths. Take into account that, whatever the theme, a few years down the road the toddler won't be a toddler anymore and will want a room that looks a lot more grown up. ✳

▼It's sleek enough to please the teen she'll become, but this room also has features the toddler enjoys right now, such as the bed enclosure with toy shelves and overhead bars for mobiles and monkeys. The window bench is a play surface now. Note the easy-access drawers under all.

▲ A garden gate can fence off an unsightly radiator and guard against burns at the same time.

Keep 'em Safe

Toddlers get into everything. Parents can't turn a toddler's bedroom into a sterile, completely risk-free environment, but they can take some simple steps to avoid potential accidents. High on the safety list are climbing-and-falling accidents and electrical cords and outlets. Because toddlers can climb shelves and open drawers, cover lower shelves with a safety fence and add a latch to low drawers so they don't become climbing surfaces. Put plug covers on every outlet, because small children will find something to stick in them otherwise. Keep cords secured behind furniture so that toddlers can't pull lamps off onto their heads or chew on cords.

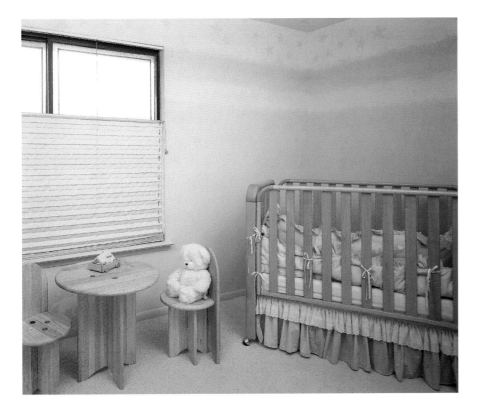

◀A painted pastel sky and perimeter rainbow soften this potentially severe room. The bottom-up shade and kid-size furniture reinforce the cozy atmosphere.

Primary Colors

Even at a young age, kids have favorite colors. They aren't necessarily the sweet pastels or primary shades automatically associated with a child's room. Wherever possible, it's important to work a bit of their favorite color or colors into their rooms. Parents who prefer a little more control should pick two or three color schemes for the room and let their child choose one. After the child has picked a scheme, the parent can decide which will be the main color and which to use as accents.

Here are some color-use rules of thumb. Bright, contrasting shades such as red, green, and yellow make for a high-energy atmosphere; softer tones are more soothing. White and light colors expand small spaces. Deep, dark colors make large rooms feel more intimate. The dark-painted cabin of the homemade locomotive bed shown at right makes a great playhouse but also contrasts nicely with the light-colored walls. Put white next to a color, and the color seems more intense. Shiny surfaces such as glossy paint or coated wallpaper reflect the light, so they brighten the room.

▲The cabin of this homemade locomotive bed makes a great playhouse. Large drawers hide under the mattress platform, and novelty drawer pulls rev up the dresser.

The Bed As Adventure

For toddlers, a bed is more than just a place to sleep. It's home base. Nestle a toddler's bed in a corner or in an enveloping cove, and make this the resting ground for a few favorite toys. When he's is ready to settle down, this cozy place will welcome him like a friend. Make the bed an adventure—perhaps with a rustic farm or fishing theme of the room at left and below, which will stimulate a toddler's imagination.

Although toddlers are a little young for bunk beds and loft beds (I don't recommend bunk beds for children younger than age six), a variety of other creative setups are suitable. Consider a bed with built-in storage, such as drawers under-

▲Enough but not too much, the rustic farm theme of this room will stimulate, not stifle, this toddler's imagination. Simple toy caddies under the bed are easy for a child to reach and use.

▶The components in this room form a well-coordinated, space-saving package. The bed, which doubles as a couch, contains deep drawers. Shelf units and a table fill every inch of wall space around the window, but light-hearted shapes and colors make them playful.

neath or built into the headboard—anything with extra spaces for a child to stash his or her favorite stuff, like the toy caddie under the bed in the bottom photo on the facing page. Color and curves coordinate furniture that was custom tailored for this room. And although the storage unit in the photo at right looks pretty grown up, it's still a neat place for a small boy's toys. He's even got built-in lights for bedtime reading.

Children this age usually don't have friends sleeping over; but for those occasions when they do, consider a trundle bed. These beds have been around for centuries in one form or another. They're pretty simple: An extra mattress platform on rollers (usually trundle beds are twin-size) fits under the main mattress and rolls out when needed. This even may be an option if two young children share a room and there's limited space. They can take turns sleeping in the pull-out bed. It doesn't take a lot to stoke a child's imagination. What little boy wouldn't love the bed shown at right? The trundle train bed rolls out for sleepovers or could be replaced with under-bed drawers if needed.

▲This storage unit looks pretty grown up, but it's still a neat place for a small boy's toys; and the style will age well as he matures. There are even built-in lights for bedtime reading. The computer table is low enough for the boy to use now, but can be raised when he gets bigger.

▼Here's a transportation storybook in furniture form. The trundle bed rolls out for sleepovers. Replace it with roll-out drawers to control clutter.

Rooms for Grade Schoolers

When kids enter school, they enter a whole new world: clubs, sports, and hobbies. Their circles of interests and friends expand. And the amount of stuff in their rooms increases. Every kid in this age group becomes a collector. Whatever the collection—shells, baseball cards, rocks—it will continue to grow. Accordingly, school-age kids need lots of built-ins, not only for their collection, but also for books, toys, craft projects, and the ribbons and trophies they will earn.

Children this age also spend a fair amount of time in their rooms, playing, doing homework, and talking on the phone. Organize the space so it has zones for each activity—homework, hobbies, puzzles. If there's no separate playroom in the house, part of the bedroom can be turned into a place where kids

▼A built-in activity center rolls into action with a desk extension and retractable cabinet doors. Even the aquarium glides out for cleaning and a better view. More storage hides behind the green door.

▲ Stencils turn a bulletin board into a colorful backdrop for photos and pictures in this altar to sports greats. Faux baseball gear hangs from fake hooks on the headboard, but the storage cubbies at the foot of the bed are the real thing.

can play with their friends. This is the place for games or crafts. Kids love built-ins with overhangs and perches that work either as play space or toy shelves are favorites.

Can a spare bed be squeezed into a child's room for sleepovers? A trundle or bunk bed makes sleepovers an adventure. Kid love climbing up to the top bunk. And starting around this age, lofts are a safe option too, and that opens up whole new possibilities.

Even for grade-school kids, school isn't just fun and games. Challenges and hard work are also part of the mix. That's why home, and especially the bedroom, takes on special value as a place to relax. A sheltered bed nook or tucked-away loft gives children their own comfortable space where all is calm. ✳

Look under the Bed

In small or crowded rooms, there are ways to squeeze out that last bit of usable space. Space under the bed is one of the first places to look for added storage. Measure the area and construct a simple box with casters to fit there. You can even find an unused wood drawer or two that fit under the bed and then screw on casters. You'll have movable storage units that glide easily in and out.

▲ Built-ins line this room from floor to ceiling; but they don't overwhelm, because they're all in a uniform, mellow shade, seasoned with bright geometrics. Toys, books, collections…everything fits neatly into shelves and cabinets.

◄ The architectural lines of the room mesh with the design of these built-in bunk beds with integral storage. There's enough shelf space for both children, plus each boy gets his own reading light.

As Close As Twins

Parents of twins know well that, even if they look alike, twins often have different personalities. The twin girls who live in this house started out sharing a bedroom and bathroom. But by the time they were nine, it was clear that each needed her own space. The remodeler built an addition to the house to give the girls separate bedrooms and baths—with a twist.

The two bedrooms are similar enough to be equal, yet not identical. One has a skylight over the desk area; the other has a window niche for the desk. The placement of closets and shelving differs to fit the different room configurations. And each girl picked the color for her room.

With separate, back-to-back bathrooms, the girls don't need to bicker over whose turn it is to use the mirror. Despite all this newfound separateness, the girls are, after all, still twins. In the connecting wall between their bathrooms is a small, glass block "window." When the girls get lonely, they can open the window to visit.

▲▲A pair of closets with louvered doors flank a window niche for this twin's desk and hanging shelves.

▲This sister didn't get a niche for her desk but she did get a small skylight. The addition that contains the girls' bedrooms also contains a good solution to sibling rivalry: Give the kids some choices and let them make some of the decisions.

Shared Bedrooms

Shared rooms can work but they work best for kids who are not so close in age that they compete, and not so different in age that they live in different worlds.

"Separate but equal" should be the guiding design principle: Each kid should get her own shelves, drawers, closet space (separate closets are best), display space, homework area—and lighting.

In the room shown below, one girl gets headboard and footboard in the shape of a house; the other, gets dimensional wall art. Twin shelves form a niche that encloses two desks.

Within the single room shown on the facing page, two kids almost have rooms of their own, thanks to the stepped cabinetry between the spaces. The double-sided unit contains counters and storage that starts high and drops to table height.

It's especially important to give each child a place to retreat and relax. A framed bed enclosure with drop curtain makes a nice private cocoon. Use half walls or low panels, folding doors, pocket doors, sliding doors, screens, or curtains. Platforms and lofts may not actually be dividers but they separate territories. If each child has all the essentials of a complete room—window, door,

▲Similar but not identical spaces hold this room together without making it at all boring. One girl gets the head and footboards in the shape of a house; the other, in tighter space, gets dimensional wall art that continues the theme.

►An S-shaped Fiberglas partition splits this not-too-large room into separate sleeping areas that share a play space. Each curl of the S doubles as a closet and a night-light. During the day, the Fiberglas lets the sun shine through.

good ventilation, light, and temperature control—the room can be split with a full structural partition. Give it a door so the kids can be together when the mood strikes. An S-shaped Fiberglas partition can split a not-too-large room into separate sleeping areas that share a play space. Each curl of the Fiberglas S in the photo below doubles as a closet and a night-light. During the day, sunlight passes through the Fiberglas.

▼With stepped cabinetry between them, the kids who share this space have complete, separate rooms. The double-sided unit contains counters and storage that starts high and drops to table height. Hand-painted graphics garnish the window shade.

▲Why stop at the window when you can create a window seat that runs wall to wall? This one, in a nook defined by ceiling molding, incorporates a bed, couch, table, and storage. The porthole window adds a sunny touch.

◄For now, niches hold picture books and the loft over the bed nook is home to a little girl's stuffed animals. When she gets older, she can use the niches for magazines and climb into the loft to talk on the phone.

Free to Explore

Nothing better symbolizes adventure and possibility than an open door. A window onto the outside world can divert a child's attention from television and computers, but a door will let the child pass through to that world. For sure, not every kid gets a bridge from the bedroom to the backyard. But if the yard is enclosed and secure, why not give the kids a door to the outside?

If planning a new house or a remodel of your existing home, parents might consider using a door to link their kid's room to the big world outside. Not only do the wide French doors in this room give the child a sense of freedom and responsibility and allow him to play in the yard when he wants. They also admit lots of light—as does the triangular gable-end window.

▲ It's not every child who gets a bridge directly from his room to the backyard. But if a yard is enclosed and secure, why not give a child a door to the outside?

The Little Room That Grew Up

Most people would ignore a second-floor space like the cramped, dimly lit room in Jim Garramone's Cape Cod–style house. But Garramone, a residential interior designer, saw it as found space, with the makings of a charming bedroom that could evolve as his daughter grew from infant to teen.

First he brightened it with four operable skylights and white paint, as shown below. Next he opened up the short exterior walls known as kneewalls and crafted cabinetry to fill those spaces. The cabinets are unpainted birch with Corian tops and back-lighted glass block strips. The style is durable, adaptable, and neutral enough to suit a nursery as well as a teen retreat. Roomy dresser drawers line one wall (shown in the bottom photo on the facing page). Large, glide-out storage bins line the other (shown below).

▲▶ Skylights, a child-size scale, and clever detailing make this half-story space the success that it is. The built-in desk tucked into the knee-wall (notice the little extra light that comes through the back-lit glass block windows), smart use of space, and abundant natural light make a room that would delight any child.

A closet without a door almost creates the sense of another room in this small bedroom. For now, the closet is an annex for bulletin board, and clothing. When the girl is older, this full-height closet will hold her clothes, which for now are in the short kneewall closets.

When Garramone's daughter was a toddler, there were three bins, all filled with toys. Now she's seven, and the center bin has been replaced by a desk and pencil drawer. As she grows older and needs more homework space, Garramone will replace the remaining two bins with drawers and more desk area; he's already wired that space for a computer.

The room has three closets—one big and two short but deep. At first Garramone installed a table and shelves in one deep closet and used it as a changing room. Now the changing table's gone and the closet is used for storage. For the time being, Garramone's daughter hangs her clothes in the two short closets. When she gets bigger, she'll shift her clothing to the tall closet—adapted once again, this time with standard-height rods (see the photo above).

▲ Why take up extra space with a chest of drawers, when the wide and deep space in the eaves of the house can hold a beautifully made built-in chest like this one. Back-lit glass blocks on this side of the room add a luminous accent.

▲A bed, desk, and drawers all under one "roof"—that's as fun as a clubhouse. Atop this one is a tented shelter that becomes an extra bunk for sleepovers. Rope vines support toy monkeys in this jungle-theme room, but they would work just as well for displays of blue ribbons.

▶Magnetic chalkboard panels split this space into play area and bedroom, providing ever-changing graphics and a wall full of fun. A counter on the back adds play space.

◄The room may come up short in floor area, but what kid would complain, with a bright, steeply soaring space like this?

Organizing Clutter

Most kids have one room in the house to call their own, their bedroom. Because so much goes on in there (homework, projects, listening to music, eating, hanging out), it's too much to expect the room to be neat all the time.

However, encourage neatness by teaching children organization. Provide them with baskets, bins, hooks, pegs, shelves, and bulletin boards. Having a place to put everything will allow cleanup to become a routine.

►A chalkboard tabletop that breaks into jigsaw-puzzle pieces performs enough functions so it can entertain several kids at once.

A Room within a Room

The ordinary kid's room never made much sense to designer Kimberly Fiterman. Things are forever brought out and put away, set up and dismantled. So she came up with an different concept for the room her two young sons share.

Fiterman built this bed structure in the center of the room, then distributed permanent, ready-to-use activity areas around the room. There's little setup, and the kids can pursue different activities without crossing paths.

The plywood and fiberboard bed structure has stone-look walls, leather gate, and crenellated top rail. The older boy sleeps on top of the structure. Inside the castle the younger boy's mattress, book nooks, and a television/VCR system is a spot for reading or watching a movie. The aquarium side houses an adjustable

▲ With it's stone-like walls, arched windows and ample built-ins, this castle-design bed structure provides private spaces for an older boy on top and a younger boy on the bottom.

desk, drawers, and computer cabinets. The aquarium allows light to penetrate the structure from this side; cutouts open it to light and air.

The room's window wall is loaded with built-ins. Window seat storage flanks a central toy box with drawers. Shelves line the narrow floor-to-ceiling corner cabinet. A three-section table drops down to form a play surface stretching from window to window. For smaller projects one or two table leaves will do. Above the central section is another table that drops down; this one has a miniature train set attached and ready to roll.

Boys' Home Is a Castle

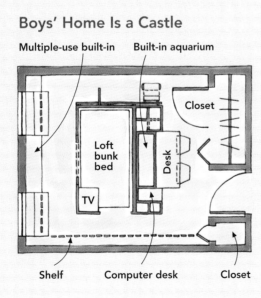

Multiple-use built-in Built-in aquarium

Closet

Loft bunk bed

Desk

TV

Shelf   Computer desk   Closet

◄A clever and versatile wall unit takes full advantage of the limited space in this New York apartment. The unit transforms from a play counter to a set for miniature trains to toy chest and storage unit to a window seat.

◄Build a whole room around a single piece of furniture. This box may be a toy chest now, but later it will store sweaters or sports gear.

◀Compose a comfortable room under the eaves using low storage against the short walls and stackable units where there's more head room. All these modules can be rearranged when your kids are ready for a change.

Skylights for Tight Spots

In rooms where there's more roof than wall, skylights are the best way to bring in natural light. There are three basic types of skylights: fixed (which don't open), ventilating (which open to let heat escape), and balcony type (which pop out to form a small balcony). Consult a windows dealer to determine the type that's right for your room.

▶Not many opportunities for natural light and ventilation exist in this attic space, where the walls are too short for ordinary double-hung or casement windows. That's why skylights make lots of sense. They're also a great choice for this toddler's bedroom because they're safe: They don't open far enough for a little one to climb through.

Almost
Teenagers

And now for the high-intensity years. You know what I mean. Kids nine or even younger officially become preteens when suddenly they decide they've got to be with friends (either in person or on the phone), must have the right clothes, and have to personalize their rooms from floor to ceiling.

Rooms for preteens are three-dimensional portraits of who they are or who they want to be. For girls, the portrait is likely to be frills and ruffles. Boys this age create dens of sports or music, dinosaurs or computers, whatever excites them.

Kids can have their room their way, and parents can make it work better for them by creating atmosphere without sacrificing practicality. In a girl's room, for example, wrap a trellised arch around the window and complete the structure with a window seat containing inset drawers. For a boy, frame the windows with lockers instead of a trellis.

▲This interesting construction divides one room into three: a study center, a sleeping area, and a perch with shelves and a cabinet nested beneath. Fun but sophisticated, the room will age well.

Preteens need space—literally and figuratively. After raiding the refrigerator, they and their friends will stampede to their room. That's why compartmentalizing the room is important. The areas where kids sleep and do homework and keep their clothes should be separate from the place where the crowd sits and listens to music. Mold that conversation niche with a soffit and partition enclosure, a lowered ceiling or a ring of built-in bench seating (which could be used as an extra bed when a friends stays over).

Junk overload can become a real issue at this stage. An expansive system of shelves, cabinets, pigeonholes, and racks—built under seats and countertops; around doors, windows, and desks; in corners and along any unused wall space—can fit into the theme of the room while helping kids keep books and magazines, CDs and videos, clothes, and accumulated stuff from taking over. ✳

▼ **Rather than paint the walls one color and the trim another, the architect/owner of this New England house chose a palette of colors that open up a small room with the help of a big round window.**

◄Preteens with all-consuming interests are happy in total-immersion rooms like this one. The wall mural and the faux-painted cabin walls create a woodland world even in the city. Fitted out with shelves, the beached canoe reinforces the theme while doing a job holding books and trophies.

▼Columns, platforms, built-ins, and beams define efficient zones and leave plenty of open space in the center of this cool room. The platform houses a bed plus a window alcove with versatile futon-like couch.

▲Cathedral ceiling, exposed beams, a skylight, and a bold red fan combine to make compelling territory for a preteen. White walls expand the room with reflected light. Storage bins or an extra mattress for sleepovers can be stowed under the high bed.

Natural Light Works Wonders

A little sunlight makes a big difference in kids' spaces. Natural light adds a spark of magic to the tiniest room or out-of-the-way corner. Cut a window opening to turn a closet into a playhouse. Pierce the roof with a skylight to create a bright attic room. Use glazed rather than solid walls to extend sunlight into interior spaces. It's not always necessary to cover windows with curtains or shades. For privacy and light, consider replacing clear glass with frosted panes.

Sleeping Over (and Under)

Loft beds make such great use of space that it's easy to understand why they are so popular in college dormitories—or anywhere space is at a premium. And whatever a loft bed can accomplish in a dorm room, it can do with much greater style in a child's bedroom.

An architect built this "room in a box" of heavy timbers to relieve the off-putting squareness of his daughter's closetless room. Now she's got a curtained closet, a bed with loft bunk, and built-in shelving.

Although a room doesn't have to be tiny to justify a loft bed, the structure will dramatically increase usable space. When company is over, the loft doubles as an extra bed. The rest of the time, the loft serves as a secret getaway or retreat.

Though fairly easy to construct, they're also for sale from many bunk bed manufacturers. Whether building or buying, there are a few things to consider. First, make sure that

◄An architect built this room in a box to relieve the off-putting squareness of his daughter's closetless room. Now she's got a curtained closet, a cozy bed with a loft bunk, and lots of built-in shelving.

◄ The curtain over the lower bunk in this loft bed rolls up and ties off out of the way. When the curtain drops, the lower bed becomes a private retreat for the girl. On top is room for a friend to sleep over.

▼ The two preteens who share this awesome room have space to spread out and up—to a loft and, above that, a cupola. The main floor is sectioned into game zone, study center, storage place, and basketball court. Alcoves notched into the wall double as reading nooks and extra beds for friends. The architect arranged the space so a wall can be built when the boys get older, splitting the room into two.

no portion of the loft is resting on movable furniture that can shift and cause the structure to collapse. Lofts should be freestanding. And don't make the loft out of pressure-treated wood. Treated lumber is designed for outdoor use only and its chemicals can be hazardous in an enclosed space.

Lofts should stand without leaning against the walls or putting pressure on the ceiling. Safety railings on top bunks are a must. If the loft is placed parallel to and up against a window, safety railings should always be installed on the window side, too.

Because houses often have different ceiling heights, be sure and measure twice before ordering a loft bed. The bed will work best if there is enough room between the top of the mattress and the ceiling so that a child can sit up in bed. The large room (shown above) is wide open, yet organized into study, storage, and play zones. The high point of the room is a tall loft that is both bed platform and gateway to a cupola.

▲ **Look for opportunities to showcase kids'
interests.** This baseball fan's bedroom uses
sporty locker room metal cabinets for storage
and a bat-studded headboard. Collectibles cover rugged faux-brick and stone walls.

◀ **Nestled under the eaves,**
this room keeps things organized by locating the built-in
desk in one alcove and display
shelves in another. The L-
shaped bunk helps segment
the open space; the lower
berth can be a couch or an extra bed for sleepovers.

Clutter Control

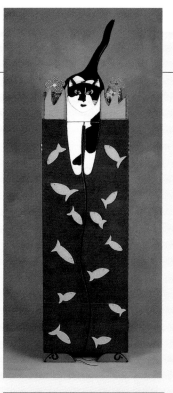

Kids' rooms are flooded with stuff. Most kids don't know what to do about it, and they don't even recognize that it bothers them. But when the chaos subsides, they feel better.

Parents can do their kids a favor by helping them control the clutter. Parents can't change their kids' personalities, but can set up a system that will harmonize with their children's habits. If a child is basically disorganized, don't expect absolute order. Instead, propose that she keep her desktop clear, or reserve one shelf for loose papers, or toss all her sports gear into one big box. For a messy kid, hooks are more likely to be used than hangers, and big containers are more practical than rows of little cubicles and shelves.

Plenty of built-in storage, including a desk and computer center, help keep this well-planned room organized (see the photo at left). The laminate cabinet system with inset desk covers one whole wall. A beam outlines a display bay at the entry, and the bathroom connects to another corner of the room.

Even young children can get organized. Ask them how they want to group their stuff—Legos in one basket, cars and trucks in another? If they pick the system, they'll probably use it. A simple bin system may be best for teens. They can pile clean clothes in one, dirty clothes in another. If all else fails—there's always the yard sale. Even a plain wood cabinet can assume a personality of its own with some imaginative application of paint and trim (photos shown at right).

▲ Durable, easy-to-clean, and affordable laminate built-ins fill out an entire wall in this bedroom, which is visually sectioned off by the perforated beams and steel posts. By building in the desk and shelving, the architect found space for a homework center.

▲ There's no limit to what a cabinet can become with a little paint and a good dose of creativity. Most preteen girls would purr over a colorful cabinet like this one.

The Teenager's Room

A teenager's room is a private domain. The quirkier, the better. They'll do a lot on their own, re-arrange or replace the furniture or paint the walls. They may expand the room upward with a platform or loft. Given the chance, they may even move—to the basement, the room over the garage, or the spare attic room with the dormer windows.

Most teenagers would love to have an apartment-like arrangement, with a bedroom, a study area, and a lounge where they can hang out with friends. A private, adjoining bath completes the package. The parent's job is to make the space safe and functional, with good lighting, heating, cooling, and ventilation; circuitry for all the electronics; a well-equipped homework center; and plenty of storage. Once that's done, parents should give kids a budget and let them take charge.

Putting the room together is one family activity teenagers will tackle with enthusiasm. Depending on

▲ A shared bookcase between floors can bridge the distance between the teens who inhabit the upstairs suite and the rest of the family.

their skills, parents can drywall or panel the attic or basement; install a skylight; wire the room for telephone and computer; and create a variety of built-ins, from shelves to seating to lofts. Craft a wall to divide up the room—maybe an L-shaped structure or one that curves around a semienclosed lounge. Build the bed into the window bay.

Carpeting will warm the space and absorb some of the throbbing of music and television (often both are going simultaneously). Teenagers should plan an ample, well-organized closet plus a liberal allotment of drawers, shelves, and bins. Even with all the storage in the world, their clothes may still pile up on the floor.

For communication, a connection such as a message board on the door is effective without being intrusive. I know one family that made communication easy by installing an intercom between the teenage daughter's top-floor room and the kitchen. The intercom was meant to monitor babies, but it can work for teenagers, too. ✴

▼ With odd angles, a cool skylight, a couple of rooms (including a music studio), and lots of privacy, this upstairs "apartment" suits a teen just fine.

Building Some Room in a Tight Spot

Space was tight at the Collins house, with two bedrooms for three daughters and no place for overnight guests. The only direction to expand the living space was up, into a not-very-big attic. But by the time Collins, a contractor, finished working magic with the space, it was the envy of the neighborhood.

Collins popped up part of the pitched roof and broadened a dormer to create most of the 290 sq. ft. The L-shaped room features both shared areas and private territory. On one leg of the L is a bed and a shared window seat that doubles as an extra bed for sleepovers (visible in the photo on the facing page).

Along the other side of the L are private bed alcoves for the other two sisters (see the photo below left). Perched over deep drawers, each alcove has a reading light, a shelf, and a curtain for privacy. Pull-down trapdoors hide shelves for personal things. And that little door on the wall connecting bunks can be opened or closed.

The three sisters share a built-in bookcase on another wall, plus a bank of display shelves. They also share the two big closets—one for long clothes and one, where the ceiling's lower down, for shirts and skirts. Tape on the rods marks off three sections.

▲Popping up part of the roof and broadening a dormer window helped transform the attic into an extraordinary room for three teenage sisters. The little door on the wall between the two bunks can be opened or closed by mutual agreement.

▼What really makes the room work is the organization of space. The father, a contractor, gave each girl a curtained berth, a set of drawers, closet space, and a reading light. Each gets the same treatment so nobody feels slighted.

Three Sisters in One Room

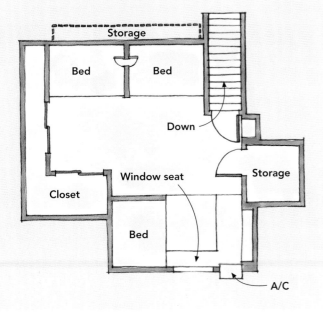

▲ Rather than create only a series of private nooks, the father also designed a common area into the room. Here, the girls can sit together, read, or have friends for a sleepover.

◀▲ Added over the garage, this room connects to the rest of the house via a short hall. Featured attractions include the high-top ceiling, the wall of adjustable shelves, and a secret place (every kid wants one) under the removable cabinet baseboard.

A Little Loft Goes a Long Way

Adults needs quiet places for retreat, so it makes sense that children do, too. Creative use of the space above closets and bathrooms that would otherwise be relegated to the dusty attic can transform a child's bedroom from an ordinary box into a place that she will treasure and use.

▲▶ Each sister got her own room and a choice of amenities. One sister opted to line the high wall in her room with display shelves; the other preferred a small loft. To maintain sibling harmony, there's a sink and vanity in each teen's bedroom.

Like Living on a Train

A tiny bedroom, 8-ft. closet, and typical teenager who doesn't hang up his clothes: For Toronto architect D'Arcy Dunal, that mix generated a great idea. He'd take his son's bed out of the bedroom—netting a little breathing room there—and build it into a closet retreat.

Dunal's son liked the sound of the plan, so Dunal rigged up a closet platform using 2x4s and slats, with a kitchen stool in front, to let the boy "try it out and see how it felt." Dunal's son loved the compactness, the privacy, the feeling of adventure.

Crafted from birch plywood, the finished retreat features a stylized Star Trek ladder and a curtained, bed-length platform. An extra few inches accommodate a headboard shelf wired for the reading light and clock radio. The "plate rail" surrounding the bed displays

◀Kid won't put his clothes in the closet? Then put him in there—after it's been converted to a room within a room. This sleeping car–style compartment features a bunk equipped with several shelves, a reading light, and curtains. Underneath is space for drawers, slide-out shelves, or, okay, a drum set.

At Home in the Closet

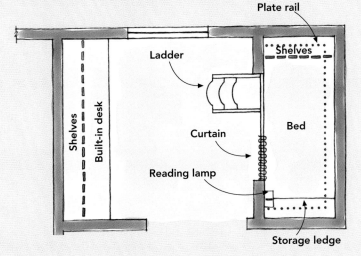

a collection of action figures—and a skateboard. Wall-mounted shelves at the foot of the bed store books. There's even room for a television. "It's pretty decadent," says Dunal.

Across from the closet, a built-in desk and shelves fill the wall. Bright-colored wire bins for socks and underwear are a lot more successful that bureau drawers.

Dunal's son is into drumming. To practice, he pulls the drum set out from under the bed. Friends sit on the ladder or pull up chairs. "It's gotten favorable reviews," says Dunal.

▲ Creative use of plywood and a bit of planning turned this ordinary closet into a secluded berth for a teenager. Shelves and reading light complete the package.

Bathrooms
for Kids

Rule number one for a child's bath is to make it safe. Rule number two: Add a bit of splash. There are so many whimsical products, fixtures, and accessories for kids' bathrooms that you don't need to settle for the ordinary. Whether you're building new, adding on, or remodeling, a child's bathroom can be enlivened easily and without major expense.

The best bathrooms not only look good but work for everybody who uses them. If two kids share a bathroom, they should have their own storage and counter space. Twin lavatories are a good way to cut down on fights over who gets to use the bathroom. A wall or even half wall between the tub area and the rest of the bathroom also lets a couple of kids use the room at the same time and still maintain some privacy.

▲ A mosaic of richly colored floor tile warms this formal, white bath like a plush carpet. The kids have separate sinks, cabinets, and mirrored cabinets; but they share an imaginative tile backsplash and ventilating windows that open right through the mirror.

If the bathroom is between two kids' bedrooms, a separate sink and toilet on each side of the bathtub space with doors on each side will give both kids privacy. Or go one step further and install a vanity and lav within each kid's bedroom.

As for the design, it's best to start with a conservative base—neutral colors and cabinetry and fixture styles that won't quickly look dated. Bright accents like a colorful laminate counter, fanciful faucets, or drawer pulls strengthen the design. A few clever tiles here and there will wake up the whole room. Buy them off the shelf or make them. Even pricey custom tiles are affordable in small quantities.

In a kid's bathroom, the accessories are key pieces of the design package. Towels, shower curtain, window covers, the wastebasket, the toothbrush holders, everything is game. Have fun, but try not to overdo it. In a small space like a bathroom, a little color and pattern are all you need. ✴

▲ It doesn't take much to make this bathroom youthful— red handles, color-flecked wallpaper, and striped shade and shower curtain. The bathroom will look just as good with more grown-up accents later.

◀The kid's touch in this sophisticated room is subtle. Steps make the vanity the right height, and cubbies keep towels handy. A partition enables two to use the room at the same time.

▼What keeps the kids' towels off the floor in this bathroom? They go on hooks, not wall-clinging towel bars. And the hooks are so big the kids can't miss when they hang up the towels.

Bathrooms: Water Safety

Anywhere there's water, there's danger for babies and toddlers. The bathroom, with tub and toilet, presents a special hazard. Because little ones can drown in a few inches of water, they should not be left in a bathroom while the tub is draining. Toilet locks, which are inexpensive and effective, keep kids out of that natural attraction. They come in either latch or adhesive styles, and while keeping out the smallest kids, they are easy for older children to use.

▲A little color goes a long way in a small bathroom. This room is basically white and blue, but colorful tiles sprinkled on the floor and wall fill the room with interest.

◀▲Two teenage girls share this classic bathroom, but each has her own basin, cabinet, drawers, and cubbies. Pale finishes augment the light from windows and skylight. The limestone counter and heated floor are both hardy and handsome. Towel cubes dot color across bonus storage cabinets and keep the towels handy by the shower.

▶The ultimate in design flexibility in a kids' bath is to "paint" the room with easily replaced accents such as towels and wall art. Stacked on shelves where kids can grab them easily, towels in rainbow colors deck out this bath. Bright fish glide across the wall.

Better Safe

A well-designed bathroom looks good, works well, and above all is safe for the kids who use it. Successful bathroom design guards against burns, slippery surfaces, and the dangerous combination of water and electrical current. This bathroom offers a variety of kid-safe details, such as the ample grab bar in the combination tub-shower, a low tub, easy-to-reach towels, and a low drawer with an insert top that allows it to double as a step up for small children. Most of the key guidelines for safe design are matters of common sense, although it never hurts to spell things out:

• **The vanity:** Make it easy for kids to reach the sink. One option is to lower part of the counter to 24 in. or so. (Later that section can be converted into storage or a makeup station.) The other option is to boost the child up with a stool or step—either freestanding or attached to the back of a cabinet door. A nifty trick designers use is to cover the bottom drawer below the sink with a solid top, turning it into a step. When the step's no longer needed, the lid comes off and it's back to being a drawer.

• **The bathtub:** Make it easy to give kids a bath. In other words, no deep tubs and no sliding doors. Install the faucet and handles off center, near where you'll be sitting when you're doing bath duty.

• **The shower:** For new construction, remodels, or additions, install the necessary rough plumbing where a shower compartment will go, even if there are no current plans for one. Later, a shower can be installed along with a privacy wall to create one bathroom that works well as a shared space. One kid can take a shower while another is at the mirror getting ready for a party.

• **Towels:** Towel bars are out; hooks and cubbies are in—just put them where it's easy for kids to use them. One designer put oval slits in the vanity apron in front of the sink in a boys' bath. The kids haven't really had to change their habit of draping towels over the sink; but now, when they stuff them through those slits, they're actually hanging them up.

▼A barrel-vaulted ceiling and top-lighted walls make this windowless room bright and cheery—and the easy-to-reach towel bars, bath toys, and vanity top should prevent unnecessary climbing. Notice how the drawer is used as a step.

Just a Few Small Touches

A child's bathroom is one of the most important rooms in the house—especially to the child. Depending on the age, a kid can spend an hour or more a day in the bathroom. Grade-school kids soak in the tub or linger and sing in the shower because it's fun. When they reach the teenage years, kids spend even more time in the bathroom—getting ready to

be seen. A little thought and planning go a long way toward making bathroom time more enjoyable and more useful, and making the room itself more durable.

Adding some special tiles is fairly inexpensive; and when the kids have outgrown the look, it's simple to remove the tiles and replace them with either a dif-

▲Some of the smiling faces that light up this bathroom are family members. The homeowners bought an assortment of cheery-face tiles at a showroom, got the name of the artist and commissioned him to pattern more tiles from family snapshots.

◄The wings of this vanity are low enough for little kids to reach the hairbrushes and toothbrushes. When the kids get older, the stepped counters will keep their bathroom stuff separate.

▼The same personalized tiles that can decorate the main bathroom can be used to lighten up standard off-the-shelf tiles in the shower enclosure. In this shower, brightly colored accent tiles reflect the interests of the children who use the shower.

ferent theme or with tiles of the same color as the rest. Or choose tiles with a look that will last a lifetime.

Durability of finish is another important factor in bathroom design. With ordinary drywall, there's always the danger of water damage or dents and dings. But in the bathroom shown above, the beadboard wainscoting—with a heavy coat of enamel paint—rises high enough on the wall to serve as a shield against such damage. And it's easy to keep clean. The same goes for the solid-surface countertop. Towels are also easy to reach and hang back up—the hooks and pegs see to that.

A Place for Everything

Most kids don't mind putting away their things if parents make it easy for them. So my advice is by all means to make it easy for them. The secret is to store stuff where it's used and to use a storage system kids understand.

By watching kids in action, parents can map out where to put the shelves, bins, and cabinets. Then shape the storage to fit what it will contain. Kids should be able to toss things into drawers and cubbies without any fancy arranging. Color-coding the storage makes it clear to kids what goes where. Show them how to straighten up the room a time or two or three, and then they'll know what to do at cleanup time.

The younger the child, the fewer the shelves, drawers, bins, and cabinets. Too many storage options overwhelm young childen. It's important to make the stor-

▲ Kids can see what's inside this basket even when it's sitting on the shelf. They can pull out the whole basket, use the blocks, then toss them back in at cleanup time.

Take a Tip from the Shakers

The Shakers were known for the rows of pegs that lined all their rooms and that kept their homes neat by holding everything from hats and coats to chairs and baskets.

Pegs are still a great idea—especially for kids' rooms. They keep things out of the way and, if they're out in the open, they promote drying of wet garments.

age simple to use—as in easy-glide drawers and smooth knobs. If kids spot something they want that's up on a shelf, they'll do whatever it takes to reach it—even if that means climbing up to it. That's a good reason to put toys on low shelves and secure storage units so they can't fall over. Covered toy boxes are great, as long as the lids have safety hinges and the boxes aren't so cavernous that stuff gets lost in the abyss.

Some storage containers can do double duty. A built-in toy bin is also a bench or step stool. A bed platform can house built-in cabinets. A curtain across a wall cavity creates a combination toy holder and play alcove. Take off the closet door and replace it with a curtain, and the closet doubles as a playhouse. ✳

▼ The stair leads to a children's suite, and this collection of cubby holes sets the theme for what's above. At varied heights, the shelves offer storage and display space for kids, from the shortest to the tallest.

Anybody Can Get Organized

If a teenager's closet looks like the one at right, try injecting some sanity into the mess. Put the basic organizing structure in place, and there's a chance that the teenager will keep his stuff organized and in view on shelves, rods, and bins instead of losing everything in a heap on the floor. Before spending the money on a complete storage system, however, take an inventory and throw out whatever can be discarded. Then separate out clothes by season and either store them in an out-of-the way place or in the back of the closet. Next, separate out the clothes the child hasn't worn in a year or so (or has never even tried on) and get rid of those. Once the stock of stuff is whittled down, get organized, like the closet shown below.

◀▲If a teenager's closet looks like the closet above, inject a healthy dose of organization and sanity. Rather than losing everything in a heap on the floor, where clean clothes mingle with clothes for the wash, shelves rods and bins installed in the closet will at least give him the opportunity to keep his things straight.

▼A junior-size armoire puts drawers and hangers at just the right height for little kids who are learning to get dressed without help. Later, shelves can replace the glide-out rod.

▲▲A closet is a closet is a closet, unless carpeting and toy shelves invite kids to use it as an extra play area. Double sets of rods and hooks use back and side walls without filling the play space.

Think Small

Almost no space is too small to be a great kid's room. Some of the cleverest and best kids' rooms are the smallest ones. If there's good light, ventilation, and adequate space for the essential furnishings, kids should love their mini-rooms.

But where will everything go? Simply put: above and below. Bunk beds, raised platforms, small lofts, and wall-mounted shelves capitalize on space in the top half of the room. Down below, slide a trundle bed under a low platform, and tuck a desk or closet under a high one.

Pick a closet system that uses every square inch of storage space. There may even be enough closet space left over for the little reading nook or play corner. This is the case in the shared bedroom on the facing page, which was created out of a hall in a small apartment. Undersize custom mattresses

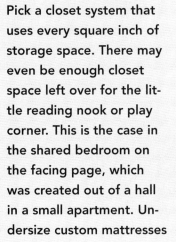

▲▶Firmly bolted to the wall, this storage system has monkey bars for live-wire kids. With a few more ladder bars and a perimeter guard rail, the cabinet roof could be used as a loft for older kids. Under the bed, wide and deep cabinets keep toys, games, and books handy.

▲Believe it or not, this hallway has been converted into a castle for two girls who live in their parents' small city apartment. Mattresses fit into the castle bed, which has drawers beneath.

tuck into the castle bed, which features under-bed drawers, video shelves, and a castle tower peephole.

For an "expandable" room, consider nesting tables, folding chairs, or a slide-out desktop. How about lazy Susan shelves for books, toys, and CDs? The storage system in the photos on the facing page, which is secured to the wall, makes the most of a small space. It even has monkey bars. With more bars and a guard rail, the top could become a loft. You can furnish your kid's room with components that also do several jobs—a wardrobe, for example, with compartments for clothes and toys, or a futon that can be a chair or an extra bed.

▶Like a jumbo curio box, these tall and narrow shelves store toys, collectibles, and books and compose them in a wall montage.

▶Everything's within reach in this adjustable shelf system. Kids can slide out the under-shelf toy baskets or use the deep base shelf as a step to upper shelves. Note the picture mounted on the wall within the shelf area.

▲Storage systems don't have to be elaborate or expensive. Clear plastic bins in assorted shapes and sizes keep toys organized yet visible so kids can find what they want, even tiny toys that would otherwise get lost.

Places Built Just for Kids

► Enfolded in a wall niche, this bed enclosure is a world apart, complete with reading lights and "window" openings. The built-in bookshelves and drawers add to the magic of this self-sufficient island.

Every house needs a special place or two where kids can do what they're meant to do: be kids. Whether it's a playroom, homework center, or some tiny niche that no adult could even squeeze into, these just-for-kids spaces are some of the most important in the home—because they're where children can freely play, explore, imagine, and learn.

The rooms and open spaces in this chapter—many illustrated with floor plans—show that thoughtful planning and creative design can turn ordinary and run-of-the-mill into useful and even beautiful. As you'll see inside, the byword for a successful kids' activity area, and good play space in particular, is flexibility. ✳

◄ Play options multiply in this room as it steps up from broad, open space to platform to cozy window nook. The wraparound rail with clear panels provides safety without blocking the sun. Wall-mounted lamps brighten the window nook and the built-in play table. Blue paint accents the storage niches.

Suites

One of the most interesting trends in modern residential architecture is the design of multi-room, suites for children in which an entire section of the house is set up for kids. These suites, which incorporate both shared and separate rooms, are proof that when it comes to space planning, the whole can be a lot better than the sum of its parts.

Children love the feeling of independence they get from "owning" a section of the house. And, designed carefully, kids' suites still give each child privacy and personal space, as the floorplans in the examples ahead illustrate. But these suites often offer even more. For instance, a Minnesota family with two sons and a daughter gave the girl her own bathroom within the suite. And although the boys share a bath, they got a secret loft hideaway that connects their rooms. In

▲ ▶ Clever use of a compact space gives two young girls separate bedrooms plus a shared loft and play landing. Slipped into a gable end, the loft has an exterior window as well as one overlooking the landing. In the bedrooms, the girls' desks fit into window niches under the loft. Velvet curtains mark the entry to the walk-in closet where both kids' clothes and toys are stored.

another home, a remodel gave two sisters a bedroom and a bath each—and access to a large attic loft that contains enough room for the two of them and a group of friends to play.

In most suites, bedrooms are not shared. Each kid may even get a private bath or half bath, which is practical from a design and construction standpoint if the bathrooms are placed back to back to share plumbing. However, the rest of the space is often shared. Bedrooms may encircle a common study area, playroom, or lounge. They may have overhead connections, such as separate entrances to a shared loft or attic room. Some suites include a place to make snacks, or a media center, or roomy built-in window seats that provide extra beds for sleepovers. Making bedrooms small conserves space that's then reallocated to make shared spaces bigger and better. ✳

Adding Light

Kids stick to an activity longer and enjoy it more if they have the benefit of proper lighting. Rooms where they play or study should have good ambient lighting, lighting that brightens the entire space evenly and without glare and leaves no areas in murky shadow.

Task lighting, or lighting that illuminates a particular area for a particular purpose, should channel the strongest light to the desktop, reading chair, play table, or other activity center. Put switches for these and all lights where kids can safely reach them.

Reading light should pour over a child's shoulder, although his or her head shouldn't cast a shadow onto the book page. Floor lamps, long-stemmed table lamps, carefully angled track lights, and wall fixtures work well.

At the desk or play table, a similar rule applies: Use nonglare lighting that angles onto the work area without shadows. Desk lighting should cover a broad enough space to illuminate books and papers spread out over the desktop. If a child can look over and stare into the light bulb when seated at the desk, the lamp is the wrong height or the shade is the wrong shape. Incandescent or halogen lighting is generally better for kids' spaces than harsher fluorescent lighting.

Room for Three Children

Three kids share this suite of bedrooms, which has both a special place for homework and a secret loft hideaway that connects the two boys' rooms. Across the way, their sister has her own separate territory.

The boys' mirror-image bedrooms are linked by semiprivate baths. The boys share a toilet and tub, but have individual vanities, cabinets, and closets. Fixed ladders from the bedrooms to their shared loft pull out for climbing up or down and push flat against the wall when not in use. The loft is big enough for a couple of sleeping bags or a bean bag chair. Between the two is a door

▶At the end of the hall that separates the girl's room from the boys' suite is a small built-in window seat with storage beneath. This is a quiet place for individual private time, for reading, thinking, or talking on the phone.

▲Each brother has his own ladder up to the shared loft that fills otherwise unused attic space between the two bedrooms. Here the ladder in one bedroom is in its "out" position.

▲When it's not in use the ladder to the loft is pushed against the wall, where its rubber feet keep it in place and prevent the floor from being marred. The ladder is fixed to the loft by metal tubing.

Kids' Suite with Loft Getaway

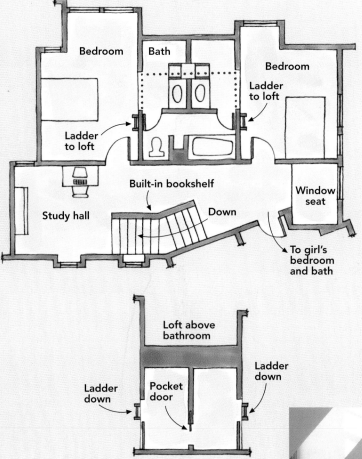

room, one son got a turret, and another son got a loft. We often use the attic space to yield a loft space and add a skylight or some other minimal source of light to capitalize on it."

In the house shown here, the broad hallway that leads to the three bedrooms features a window niche, with comfortable seat and built-in drawers, for quiet reading. The stairwell is lined with built-in bookcases. At the other end of the hall is a secluded study area with desk and a separate bookcase. Though they share the space, these three kids can find a quiet, out-of-the-way place where they can concentrate on homework.

that the boys can close whenever they've seen enough of each other.

The loft is built just over the bathroom in what easily could have been useless attic space. Minneapolis architect Dale Mulfinger, who designed the house, has created several such spaces over the years for his clients with children. So even when a space may seem too small for practical use, it usually can accommodate a little hideaway. "We try to make each child's bedroom unique so they're not just 10 by 12 boxes," said Mulfinger. "On a recent house with three children, the daughter got a suite with a bath-

▲The stair landing expands the hall at one end, creating a enough room for two desks and bookshelf. Windows that peek into the landing and stairwell help flood the space with natural light.

Sisters Share a Suite

Before the remodel, the two young girls of the house each had a bedroom of her own but shared a bath and a small loft. They still share the bath but now each has her own half bath; a larger bedroom; and separate stairs to a sky-lighted loft that's big enough for both girls and some friends.

The footprint of the bedroom suite, which was expanded out over the family garage, was enlarged both up and out. Dormers were added along with room for two full staircases—one from each bedroom—to the triangular loft above, which is roughly 18 ft. by 12 ft.

▲The loft everlooks each bedroom, which is reached via a personal staircase. Although the girls share a tub and shower area downstairs, each bedroom now has a half bath with vanity and toilet.

▲The girls' bedrooms are separated by a wall. Doors to the connecting hall are open or closed, depending on the girls' moods.

Sisters' Suite Includes a Loft

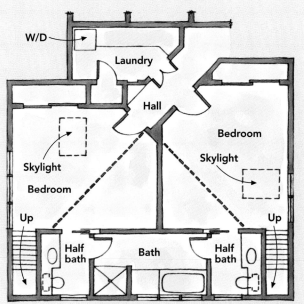

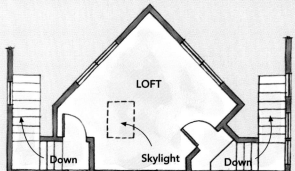

▲ The triangular-shaped loft is open to both bedrooms via a staircase. A sliding window opens onto each bedroom, creating a balcony effect. The loft receives light from the sliding windows, a skylight, and a row of halogen lights suspended form the ceiling.

Playrooms

A playroom is the place where it's always okay for kids to climb, roll and tumble, make noise, create a mess, and move things around if they want. Great playrooms can handle it. They're playful in design and rugged enough to play hard. These rooms should be alive with possibilities. Even if the space is basically a rectangle, there are lots of ways to make it a stimulating play center.

In some of the examples that follow, play spaces were part of the plans for new construction or a remodel. In other cases, such as the second-floor playroom an Atlanta architect created for his children, existing space that was too small or too eccentrically shaped was recognized as a great place for kids to play.

Children don't have to have architecturally beautiful places to play. Often, they can remain happy for hours with a cardboard box and some markers. But because kids love quirky spaces to crawl inside or climb atop, something that's well

◄ Recessed lights and a bank of skylights turn a long, narrow attic into a versatile play space. The low ceilings are an advantage here because they add to the sense of adventure.

▲ This structure organizes the room into zones: video and storage center on one side, art area on another, big blocks on a third. The rooftop rest area has a lighted niche for reading. Several kids can cluster inside the house, or one can work at the built-in desk. Little details like the operable mail slot delight kids.

► Inside the house within a house is a child-size living room with L-shaped sofa, built-in shelving for toys and games and a little table with chairs. For young kids, the room is big enough for tea parties or even birthday parties.

built and carefully designed can provide them with years' worth of entertainment. And if done right, the play space can adapt to a growing child's changing interests.

Something as simple as a lighted closet with a curtained doorway invites kids to play make-believe. Structures with peep holes, steps, slides, passages, snug interiors, and lofty towers make a child's eyes light up— like the cartoonish play space a Nebraska architect created for two children in Omaha (see the photo on p. 98). Even in a compact room, several play levels can be incorporated— often two for one. Construct an elevated platform, for instance, and add a tunnel or niche underneath. Build a loft, maybe a carpeted one with a lookout post. The overhead loft creates a sheltered cove for a book nook, playhouse, pretend kitchen, or dress-up center. Either the loft or the cove could be the perfect getaway place for a child who wants time alone. ✳

The Secret of the Hideaway

Children love hidden, secret spots where they can hide out with other kids. They love a place where parents can't fit and don't belong. A playhouse is such a spot, where children are in charge and where their own little society is the dominant one. Though playhouses are great for small groups of kids, they're also important places for children to be alone and solitary.

▲A lot can be said for sunny play space. Kids can play separately at the wraparound activity table—or stretch out on the floor for a round of checkers or backgammon atop the painted-on rug.

▶A partial wall with overhead platform turns a basic box into a room filled with play possibilities. Along with the loft, the structure adds a cozy under-loft play space, shelving, and a reading corner. Even the railings combine function and fantasy.

▲Don't fight quirky spaces, capitalize on them. Here, odd angles make playful storage triangles, and wraparound benches form inviting, space-saving seating. Extending the seating platform to the window creates a snug retreat. To prevent fingerprints on painted drywall, install wainscoting, as was done here.

Odd Spots Are Prime Real Estate

Whether it's under the bed, in a discarded cardboard appliance box, behind the couch, or under the kitchen table, children immediately take to the quirkiest little nook or corner. The space doesn't have to be designed as a hideaway for children to enjoy it. Makeshift getaways created within low attic kneewall spaces, in dormers, window seats, little-used closets, or under-counter spaces, can quickly be transformed into a favorite spot for kids.

House within a House

A basement remodel was the genesis of this interesting play space, which blends wit with realism to allow the children who play here to run their own make-believe household.

Lori Krejci, an Omaha, Nebraska, architect, was asked to do something with a basement that had a particularly high ceiling. "So what do you do with that odd space down there?" she asked. Krejci sat down with her "little client"— a five-year-old girl—"and we started scribbling. When I finished the drawings, she colored the one she wanted and gave that one a smiley face."

▶ Just high enough for adventure but not so high that safety is a concern, the upstairs of this quirky playhouse gives children an enjoyable sense of height and enjoyment in an otherwise unremarkable basement remodel.

The chosen one was a house within a house. "The downstairs has a living room to watch TV and a kitchen space. Upstairs has a bedroom to put your dolls to sleep and play dress-up. And whenever any little kid sees it, the first thing he or she does is to run to the door, go all the way to the top and wave out at the parents." To get down, the kids take the yellow slide from the top window.

Creating a space within the house that's higher than everything else gives children a new perspective. "Like an adult when you stand up on a step stool in the kitchen, it changes the way you see the space."

Apart from the basement structure, the playhouse is a façade with some carpeted wood platforms inside. "It's very minimal. And once inside it can be a space ship or a pirate ship or a hospital," said Krejci.

▲ Scaled to take advantage of an ordinary basement space, this Peewee-Hermanesque playhouse with slide escape is cartoonish enough to be fun but real enough to function well for all types of make-believe. The architect created the drawings (right) and asked the children to color in their favorite parts.

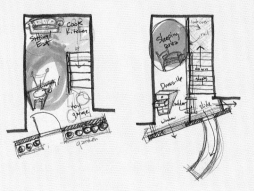

▲Blending wit with realism, this creative play space lets kids go through the motions of running a household. The cabinet doors, oven, and refrigerator open, and the television is the real thing.

◄This room invites kids to take up the jungle theme or simply to enjoy the space. The room is loaded with clever ideas: Bookcases became toy shelves with windowed, African mask doors. Other toys fit behind a wooden screen. Kids can pin their art on the flat fiberboard treescapes. The durable vinyl floor incorporates a game board and paths to play zones.

▲Long and narrow as a freight train, this skylighted attic space is the perfect venue for—a train. The cars along the kneewall make the toy cabinets fun.

▲▲A little bit of thinking like a child transformed the shallow edge of this attic playroom into a meeting place for little ones. The gabled ticket office at the stair rail doubles as a playhouse.

A Bit about Kneewalls

A kneewall is a short wall built to create usable attic space where the roof descends to the floor, or in 1½-story houses, it's the low space where the roof rests on the outside wall. It's often no higher than a few feet and often overlooked as functional space. But kneewall space is just the right height for kids.

A Room Sized for a Child

In 1994, when their first child was still a baby, Atlanta architect Phil Harrison and his wife bought a 1920s one-story bungalow with an unfinished attic. A second-floor addition on the back of the house would give the couple the room they needed. However, the attic space in the front gable end with its steeply sloped ceiling remained empty and unused, too small for any practical adult uses. Because it was so small, Harrison decided to make it a room for kids.

"It's a kid-size space, with a low ceiling. It's captured space," said Harrison. "This was originally nothing, just empty attic space. And we wanted to preserve that gable because it adds nice architectural character to the front of the house."

Now a new stair goes up to a second floor and to a partial third floor, which contains an office. There's an 18-ft. ceiling in the stairwell and big windows at the top that bring light into the stair and second floor. At the second-floor landing, behind French doors, is the playroom

"It could've been a nursery or a small home office. The ceiling height at center is about 8 ft.," Harrison said. "But a desk would've had to be in the middle of the room." Instead, Harrison dug into the short kneewall for space for a computer desk and drawing table. On the other side of the room is recessed cabinetry.

The windows in the gable, which are replacements, have a "very low sill, so they're proportioned to a child," Harrison said. "The room has double doors, which we leave open. It feels more like an extension of the stair space, which is completely open to the downstairs level where we can hear the kids quite well."

▲ Just off the stair landing and within earshot of parents, this formerly unused attic space in a remodeled bungalow just happened to be the right size for a young boy's playroom. Later, when he's older, the low kneewalls can become storage areas while the full-height section of the room could serve as a studyhall or media room.

▶ The right size for the child, but way too short for the parents, this shallow attic space seems custom-made for a play center.

▼The ceiling soars and the playroom is big, but this converted garage off the kitchen manages to feel friendly and warm. How? Built-ins bring the focus down to a more intimate scale, and the clouded-studded sky unifies all the components in one continuous wash of whimsy.

▲ Standing in the kitchen, mom can keep an eye on the toddlers as they play in this converted garage. A short bit of wooden fencing ensures there are no strays.

▶ The remodeler raised the garage floor to eliminate the step up into the house and added a window bay that brightens the room. The bay window works as a hideaway for children or as a cozy spot for the adults to pull back and watch the kids play.

Hideaways

Hideaways are eternal. All kids gravitate to kids-only alcoves where their imaginations can soar. For me it was the special place I created by draping a cloth "house" over a card table. For my daughter it was the cardboard box—with cutout door and window—in which our washing machine was delivered. The best hideaways are tucked into out-of-the way places where kids can enjoy a sense of intrigue and adventure. Let the children help find the spot and design the perfect hideaway.

One reason kids like—and need—small hideaways is that most of the time they feel dwarfed in a big people's world. In their own little space, particularly one with a low ceiling, they feel secure—masters of their own small territory. A cavity under the stairs, found space under an overhang, a pocket of space under the eaves, almost any niche can be transformed into a wonderful kid cove. A Minnesota architect, whose work is shown

◀▲Though meant to be a closet, this space is more fun as a secret room behind a concealed door. Reoriented to open over the stairs, it's reached via steps notched into the wall; the flowers on the hedge form a railing of sorts. One important addition is the porthole window, which keeps the room from feeling like, well, a closet.

on p. 107, routinely mines unused attic space for little hideaways.

A loft instantly becomes a favorite hideaway, especially if it has the makings of adventure, such as a ladder, private window, or interior lookout. A mini-loft can be built into a closet. In fact, just a curtain or pocket door can transform a simple closet or odd corner into a fun hideaway. When its hideaway days are over, use the space for storage.

Hideaways aren't just for young children, and they aren't always small. Some great hideaways for older kids are magical because they are secret. One teenager has taken over the small room next to his bedroom. He's decked it out with a mattress and a stereo and sleeps there.

What kid wouldn't love a passageway between rooms? Or a room hidden behind a door that's disguised as an ordinary bookcase? Designer Alice Busch hid a preteen girl's clubhouse behind a bulletin board door with a touch latch. It's carpeted, lighted, and fitted out with a CD player and neon markers that the girl and her friends use to write on the walls. Not to be outdone, the girl's brother also has a secret room. Although his room has an awkward, narrow shape, it's still a winner, and shines with glow-in-the-dark stars on a navy blue ceiling. ✳

▼ Like magic, the bookcase opens to reveal a kid's bedroom. Of course, the idea works just as well if the bookcase door conceals nothing more than a small hideaway. Just make sure the room has ventilation and light and that the door opens easily from both sides.

◄Enfolded in a wall niche, this bed enclosure is a world apart, complete with reading lights and "window" openings. The built-in bookshelves and drawers add to the magic of this self-sufficient island.

Built-Ins Brought to Life

What's a better hideout than a built-in bed? Thoughtful design, a bit of paint-grade wood, and custom features—like lighting, shelving, and under-bed storage—combine to form the ultimate child's getaway. It provides privacy, a feeling of shelter, and, if done well, adds beauty to a room, much in the way a piece of fine furniture does.

▶This wall structure divides two kids' rooms and multiplies the play stations. From either side, the kids can wiggle across the upper deck of the pass-through. Each has an exclusive hideaway underneath.

A Last-Minute Loft

Sometimes, the most interesting things in life happen on the spur of the moment. Like the little loft play area in this child's bedroom. It didn't cost much money. It didn't take up much room. It wasn't even part of the original working drawings for the house. But to the child who gets to enjoy it, this little overhead space represents more enduring fun than a week at Walt Disney World.

The loft that surrounds this child's bedroom is built into a tiny bit of space pulled from attic and overhead space that, on the original plans, was empty. Architect Dale Mulfinger and the clients put their heads together as the house was going up and agreed that something could, indeed, be done with the space.

Looking through the doorway into the hall, it's clear that the ceiling height just behind the door drops down. The loft was created by lowering the ceiling height around two sides of the room. At the top of the ladder, the loft is big enough for a desk and chair. The raised part of the loft that leads to the little square opening above the door.

"A child can crawl up into that space and look out over the room, bomb a friend with a water balloon, or whatever. It wasn't a big expense. Just mining the space. A result of last-minute thinking during construction."

Exploiting Hidden Space

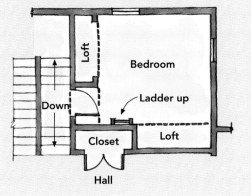

▲ From the boy's bedroom, this ladder reaches up to an L-shaped loft that includes an opening above the door.

▲It could've been just a bedroom with an ordinary bunk bed, but the parents of this lucky child held out for more. By elevating the bed (which is secured in place) on top of the chests of drawers, the designers produced a low-height hideaway for a child in what otherwise would have been an ordinary room. This arrangement works great for the child and also conserves space in this city home.

A Hideaway with Hidden Entrances

The best hideaways have secret entrances, and this one has a pair of them. Two brothers share a tiny playroom—hidden behind camouflaged doors—that was created from a bit of attic space between the older boy's bedroom and a playroom. The door to the hideaway from the bedroom side is an old gym locker. A low door in the tree trunk leads to the hideaway from the playroom.

Terri Ervin of Decorating Den Interiors in Dacula, Georgia, built this little nook for her two sons. "The room with the tree is an attic space that we finished out for a playroom. Between that and the bedroom there was a little pocket that we turned into a playhouse, or a cubby hole," she said. "It's really a tiny little

▲ It's not the home of the Keebler elves, but it's just as magical. The little door camouflaged in the tree trunk leads to a secret hideaway between two brothers' bedrooms.

place, about 8 ft. by 8 ft. square. The ceiling's about 4½ ft. high at the high end and only about 2 ft. at the low end," because of the slope of the roof.

Ervin and her husband went to an architectural salvage shop in Atlanta and found the old high school gym locker. "It just happened to fit between the 16-in. studs of the wall, and the angle of the roof cuts the opening, so it's not even a full-height door."

And never underestimate the allure of a secret getaway, no matter what age the child. Ervin and her husband created the space when their children were younger. "My son is 15 now and he sleeps in there. He's got a nice room that's about 12 ft. by 17 ft., but that little cubby hole is where he sleeps now." Fortunately, he has electricity and air-conditioning. "He has a stereo in there and a telephone and a fan. And he keeps his brother locked out of it."

▲ The gym locker door leads from the other bedroom to the secret room, which is only about 8 sq. ft. and 4½ ft. high, though it's equipped with electricity and air-conditioning.

◀Tucked under the pitched roofline, this space in a playroom became a hideaway instead of the closet it was supposed to be. The porthole is used as often as the doorway to crawl through and haul toys in and out. The cut-out moon lets the sun shine in. Everything's indestructible, from the laminate color surfaces to the shatterproof outdoor light fixture inside.

▼An odd space under a basement stairway makes a great kids' hideaway. All those jogs in the ceiling form cozy and open areas. The half-door here serves two purposes: It lets in air and sunlight and creates a puppet theater.

Look for the Nooks

Kids automatically gravitate to hideouts and nooks. If there's a closet that's not needed for clothing or a pantry not needed for canned food, take a look at the area and see what kind of space for children it can become. A door and a few shelves can transform an out-of-the-way space into a child's magical hideout.

▲An under-stair closet like this is too low for hanging clothes, but it makes a great play space. Dutch doors set the stage for a puppet show or other make-believe play. Children will love hiding out and playing in the sharp little corners of this space.

Places to Do Homework

The best homework help parents can give their kids is to provide them with a well-planned study center—a place where the kids can concentrate on their work and complete it in comfort and without distractions.

First, consider the location. Try to put the study area where distracting sights and sounds are at a minimum. Homework almost always loses in the battle for atten-

▼This built-in ensemble blends in because it matches the architectural details of the room. The countertop edge echoes the window trim, the bookcase and crown moldings match, and the wainscoting continues under the desk and behind the bookshelves. Even the edges of the bookshelves mimic the window base.

tion with television or household activities. Yet, some kids quickly become fatigued if all they have for visual relief is a blank wall. These kids need a window view. And some kids concentrate best with music or a modicum of noise in the background. The key is to suit the particular child's study habits.

Once the location is set, focus on function. Arrange the study area so that it's convenient and comfortable for kids. Give kids ample desk area so they can spread out their work. An angled, drawing board–style surface makes a comfortable place for reading and writing. If they have a computer in the study area, allow appropriate space for all the equipment.

With a little imagination, almost any space can become a decent homework center. A Denver architect made a comfortable study for two sisters out of a large second-floor landing. Wide upstairs hallways, landings, and other overflow spaces also work well. Some kids have desks in their bedrooms, but head for the family computer center when they need to type a paper or do research online. ✳

▲ A playful work center sounds like a contradiction in terms, but here's proof that the two are good partners. The witty mix of storage—topped off by the roof and oversize pigeonhole—make this homework center the highlight of the room. It's still practical though, with file drawers and reference shelves next to the desk. The corkboard displays art now; later it can hold maps and the periodic table.

The At-Home Study Hall

A dding a second story onto a one-story ranch house was a typical challenge for Denver architect Doug Walter. At 2,000 sq. ft., this ranch house—home to a family with two daughters—needed enlargement. So the 1,000-sq.-ft. second-story addition Walter designed provided lots of options for the family.

"We were looking originally to put everybody upstairs," said Walter. "Then we thought we'd put the parents upstairs. But they already had a very nice suite downstairs, so it worked out that the two girls moved upstairs with a floor of their own."

Now the second story contains a suite in which each girl has her own bedroom and bathroom. And for a commons, or study area, Walter saved a large chunk of open space at the top of the stairs.

"It's a very oversize landing, really, big enough to be a room," he said of the 10-ft. by 16-ft. area. The space contains

▲There's room in this landing for a study center and an inviting windowseat. The two sisters who share this area each gets a desk of her own, with bookcases, separated by a cushioned window seat.

a wraparound desk and a couple of computer stations and is open to the stairwell so the parents can keep tabs. Windows on three sides provide ample natural light. The large desk area contains space enough for each girl to have her own place to study or work on the computer. Separating the two is a built-in window seat for reading and relaxing.

"The tricky thing about designing spaces for kids is that they don't stay kids," Walter said. "The window seat was our nod to the kids curling up with a book. This is also a space that can grow with them. And when the girls are older, the parents will use this space. This is a southeast corner and gets wonderful sun throughout afternoon. The window seat separates the desks, but also creates a very attractive space. Everybody loves a little space like this."

Room to Share

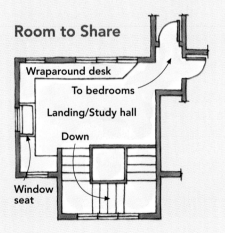

Wraparound desk

To bedrooms

Landing/Study hall

Down

Window seat

◄A compact work space takes on the appeal of a clubhouse here. The window niche has a computer; a bank of bookshelves; and for extra elbow room, a wraparound desk.

◄A built-in bed stashed in a kneewall upstairs in this timberframe home makes good use of a shallow space, and frees a full wall for full-height use, such as the built-in desk, which looks into the treetops. The study center features plenty of storage space and a big work surface. The built-in headboard shelving and under-bed storage take advantage of space that otherwise would be unused.

▼The ladder in this child's playroom/library adds a touch of elegance to the space. The bookshelves also double as display space for the children's artwork or crafts.

▲Homework and play areas on both sides of these open adjustable shelves share sunlight and access to the books—but reserve a little privacy too. A library ladder on a horseshoe track puts high shelves within reach.

Special-Activity Rooms

I f space is available and the kids are passionate about a particular activity, give them a special room custom-tailored for what they like doing best, whether it's putting on a show on their own home stage or playing basketball indoors.

Even a very small room can be turned into an arts-and-crafts studio. All that's needed are work surfaces, an organized repository for supplies, and a place for completed or in-progress projects. Provide good lighting—including, if possible, windows or skylights. A small sink comes in handy for washing paintbrushes

▼Art supplies stay organized and accessible in see-through bins nested into a wall of custom-size laminate shelving. The table is easy-care laminate, too, and is broad-sided to make room for several kids to work together. A generous spread of recessed fixtures evenly lights the activity area.

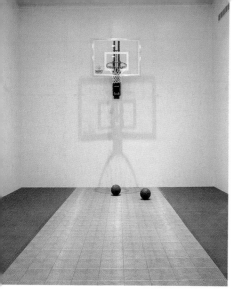

◄A basketball court was high on the wish list when the new home for a family with two boys was built. With its two-story height and plasticized rubber gym floor, the room is safe and durable.

and cleaning up. Laminates and vinyl flooring are easy to maintain.

The best place for a music room is the basement, attic, or any place that's removed from the living spaces. No matter which room you choose, line it with carpeting, extra wall insulation, and acoustical tiles to keep the sound from penetrating into the rest of the house.

Kids into sports? A smooth concrete, vinyl, or wood floor paves the way for in-line skating, street hockey, or indoor soccer. Add hoops for a basketball court. Bars for a dance studio. Mats for a gymnasium. These sports arenas are easily revamped if the kids become fans of a different activity. ✳

▼Plywood backboards and a clever paint job on the concrete floor—that's all it took to transform this basement into an indoor hockey rink. The lights are recessed, out of the way of sticks and pucks. The kids have their own stairs to the kitchen, so they can grab a snack without crossing through the living room. This room will become a teen getaway when the kids get older.

A Home Stage

A stage with track lights and sound system is just the ticket for kids with dramatic flair. The setup includes a costume closet with entries from the stage and the side. Adding to the drama, these kids also have a tunnel under the stairs.

Madison, Wisconsin, architect Bob Bouril designed the house. "This stage and play area were very important parts" of what the mother wanted, he said. "There was a great deal of emphasis on children and their having their own play area separate from the adult area. The kids are in a finished basement with walkouts. We worked in lots of storage area for toys. There's a stage and area for a projector. The mother was really involved in this, and she envisioned the kids putting on plays and acting. She's a very good mom."

Bouril said the space under the stairs wasn't practical for much. "There's only about 4 ft. of clearance, but it makes a great little play space for kids. So we added doors on either end. The tunnel leads from the playroom to the hall where the stairs are."

By doing a little planning and budgeting just a bit extra, an otherwise ordinary space became something quite special. Bouril estimates that costs for such a project—stage and storage—would add about $10 to $15 per sq. ft. to the cost of the affected area. "You can do a basic platform for less, but once you get into flooring, carpeting, and electrical, you get to that range."

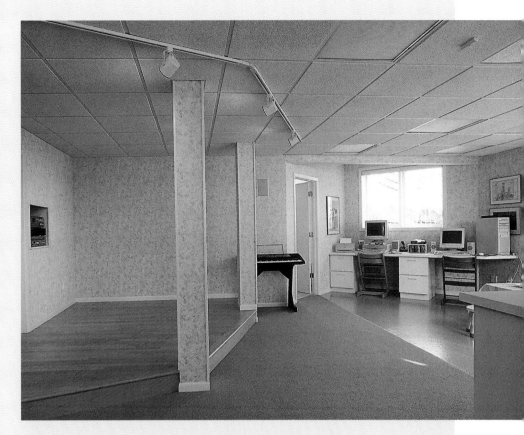

▲All the basement's a stage for the children who live in this house. Most of the basement is given over to this down-home stage, though there's room for desks, computers and other equipment. The basement also has its own secret tunnel, which leads from the hallway, under the stairs, and into the playroom.

◀It would be a stage mother's dream to have a stage at home for impromptu performances or just hamming it up. Built behind the stage in this basement play center is a well-organized costume room, with entrances onto the stage or out into the playroom.

Room for Just about Anything

◄It's a big decision to hand over so much room to indoor play. But in areas of the country where the weather is extreme or extremely unpredictable, such a space can mean the difference between kids being active and physically involved or sitting and watching television.

▼Overlooking the gym is a sort of loggia area where parents can keep an eye on what's happening below or where younger children can watch bigger kids act up on the court.

This upstairs–downstairs plan connects the two activity rooms visually and washes both rooms in sunlight. Lined with toy cabinets, the more intimate upstairs room is just right for games and other sedate play. The rugged two-story-high downstairs gym, with a whimsically painted wood floor, is ready for much more lively pursuits. Toy garages store tricycles and sports equipment under the upstairs room. On sunny days, the activity can spill into the adjacent enclosed yard.

Give Kids Space for Music and Art

Parents can spend fortunes to indulge their kids' latest interests. The problem is that such an approach can be expensive and futile—kids' likes and dislikes change often. So before pouring a lot of money and effort into a music room or a pottery room, figure out a place in the house to give the hobby a test run.

▲Everything related to music is packed into one compact area: piano, CDs, CD player, and speakers, which are on built-in shelves set into the wall. Whether it's practicing scales on the piano or listening to the latest music, it can all happen here.

▶If there's a mess to be made, kids can do it safely—and keep it contained—in this dedicated crafts area. Broad shelves display completed projects and works in progress.

Rooms for the
Whole Family

In the old days, children were allowed into the formal areas of the house only briefly and then kept out of sight. Times have changed, yet in a lot of homes today, children still are rarely heard—or even seen. That's because families today are home less and spend less time together around the table for a meal, let alone for conversation.

The good news is that more parents are grabbing hold of the time they do spend with their kids. They're welcoming kids—toys and all—into the living spaces, so the family is together as much as possible. They're incorporating kids' activities into the planning of every shared space in the house. Thanks to this enlightened approach, kids are now welcomed and ac-

▶ Built into a cozy alcove, this bench structure has just about everything a kid could want—soft seating, a window, shelves for toys and books, and even a little TV.

◀ A prominent display area for the children's arts-and-crafts projects dominates this informal Southwest-style family room; it makes the children feel proud and welcome.

commodated. It's a giant step forward in practical home design.

Ideally, family spaces and kids' spaces in the home should be linked so kids can move from place to place without crossing into parents-only territory such as the master bedroom. The kids' bedrooms and playrooms should flow into hallways that lead to the family room, kitchen, eating area, bathroom, computer center, porch, patio, front door, and backyard. In fact, hallways aren't just conduits from one room to another; they can make great kids' areas themselves.

►This hallway, which connects the master suite to the rest of the house, is an appropriately private space to display the children's arts and crafts efforts.

▼The children are out of the kitchen but not out of sight when they play in this family room. These low cabinets make it easy for small children to tuck away their toys.

Setting Up Some Boundaries

Architectural elements can subtly but very effectively organize large family areas into smaller sections. The nice thing about them is that they can help segment the space without sacrificing light, views, or flexibility.

Low ceilings, half-walls, columns, enfolding soffits, step-down areas, targeted lighting, and even such details as varied floor and wall treatments define different sections of a family room. Use French doors to enclose a sunny alcove or the area where the media system is set up. The doors will provide sound control and lend a little extra privacy.

Need a place to display Grandma's antique porcelains? Want a safe spot for your glass coffee table? It's fine to reserve part of the family space for adults. Just decide what area is off limits for high-flying kids, and clearly define that territory so nobody is confused. Choose an area that is out of the center of things, and mark the boundaries with furniture, plants, or other objects. In exchange, give the kids a place that's exclusively theirs—a well-stocked play corner where nothing is breakable and there are always plenty of things for the kids to do.

In the flow of rooms, it's best to connect the kitchen and family room, as you'll see on p. 133. A comfortable, inviting family room that's removed from the kitchen may end up defeating its own purpose, isolating the kids who congregate there after school while Mom or Dad is busy fixing dinner elsewhere.

Like shared bedrooms, the most successful family spaces are open areas organized into zones. Some zones foster togetherness; others accommodate independent activities. Some can do both, like the home on p. 130. A roomy space with a cluster of comfortable seats is just the spot for family and friends to grab a bite or watch a movie together. ✳

Family Rooms

The family room is one of the most-used rooms in the home today. It's where everybody can relax; sink into a chair; munch a snack; and talk, read, bring out the Scrabble board, watch television, or do nothing in particular. Family rooms are often open to the kitchen and dining areas and work with them as a unit of space, creating a smoothly functioning family area, like the one in the Minnesota home shown on p. 130.

Cabinets are one of the secrets of a neat family room, because family rooms accumulate clutter. But even a room that's full of stuff can look spick-and-span when the cabinet doors are closed. Nobody needs to know that they're full of toys, games, art supplies, and videos. Reserve low shelves and drawers for kids to use, and locate these kids' cabinets where they'll be handy.

▲ Elegant opened or closed, this wall of built-ins contains a complete entertainment center, with shallow, glide-out toy drawers, a television, and a VCR. The cabinet doors glide into pockets so they're out of the way.

Look in the Walls for Extra Space

The interior walls of every home, which have 2x4 studs spaced 16 in. apart (except for walls that contain plumbing or heating ducts, which are 2x6), hold room for inset shelving. To make sure there are no wires or pipes in the way cut a 4-in. by 4-in. peephole before cutting out the drywall for the shelves.

The family computer center can occupy a large closet in the family room. Open the closet, extend the pull-out computer shelf, and parents and kids are ready to do their homework. Close the closet door and the office is out of sight. When children get tired of the games and the videos, let them work off their pent-up energy in an indoor space where they can run around and play under supervision. Take a look at the indoor track idea on p. 129 that one architect came up with. ✳

▲▶A pair of wall niches, nicely trimmed out with ornamental molding, keep the family's video library neat, organized, and close to the television cabinet. The low shelves are reserved for kids' movies.

◄▲For a family that likes to entertain, this gracious room addition is ideal. It connects to the dining room via glass doors so the adults can keep an eye on things in the family room as they chat over coffee. In one corner, the kids can watch videos. In another, they can play computer games. The bottom portion of the computer cabinet houses toys and art supplies. The whole family can be in the room at the same time, doing different things without getting in each other's way. There's even a full bath that's nice enough for guests yet right next to the room's patio doors so the kids can wash up when they come in from the backyard.

An Indoor Track

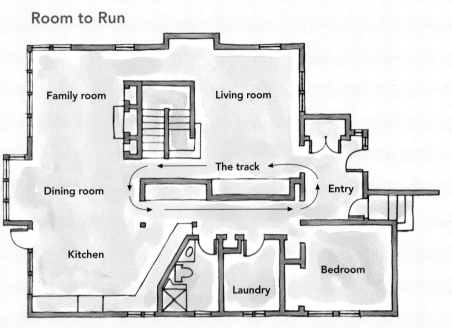

Room to Run

Family room

Living room

The track

Dining room

Entry

Kitchen

Laundry

Bedroom

Parents know what it's like to have kids cooped up inside because the weather outside is too hot or too cold or too wet: Children have energy to burn, and they're going to burn it any way they can. The way to let the kids spend all this energy without forcing their parents to use up all theirs keeping them in control? Give the kids room to move.

North Carolina architect Sarah Susanka, author of *The Not So Big House*, advocates planning an indoor track into a family home. "Especially in climates where kids can't go outside a lot in winter, they burn up with energy. There's no place to go and parents are constantly telling them to calm down, be quiet, sit down," Susanka said. "If a house has a built-in loop like the one in the drawing here, kids automatically gravitate to it as a race track. If there's a place where they can run around and hide and wait for another to come around, they do it automatically. It's a way to let them literally unwind in a situation where it's difficult because they can't race around outside."

It might seem that giving kids a large open space—say a recreation room—would satisfy the kids' urge to zip around. Susanka says square footage is not enough. In this plan, designed by Susanka's former partner Dale Mulfinger, a wall of storage running through the middle of the main level of the house provides the children with a track. "It's different if there isn't that obstacle there," she said. "Part of the delight is to get up a head of steam and hide. Like peekaboo. The fact that you're hidden for half the length is a big part of how it works. Some people would just think they've got a big wide open basement, so surely that's better. But if you put something in the middle of that open space it's even better. You need a wall; but it doesn't work if it's attached to another wall at one end because that makes a U, which defeats the purpose.

"If you think about a racetrack, you can think the same way. The fact that the path is defined makes it something that you can challenge yourself against yourself or against a friend."

Planning around Children

Most architects remember the time not long ago when families considered the main shared rooms of the house as places where kids were not quite welcome. "We thought of these rooms as places that kids shouldn't be in unless they were very well behaved," says Michaela Mahady of Minnesota's SALA Architects. "Now it's changed. Maybe it's that people want to be more involved in their children's lives. That's not to say it wasn't that way before, but now they're designing houses around them."

The first-floor plan of this Minnesota home (on the facing page) shows just how much times have changed. Here, kids are integral to the whole house plan.

For instance, the stairway spills right down into the kitchen. "A typical formal pattern would be to put stair near front entry," Mahady said. "The owners wanted the stair to go right into the kitchen where the mother is all the time. We made a broad landing so the children

▲ Low coat hooks by the back door and a concrete floor make a very functional and durable entry for kids. The pass-through to the kitchen means that grimy children can pick up a snack without tracking dirt into the kitchen.

▶ A built-in bench with under-seat storage becomes the favorite place in the house because it's in the middle of everything: between the kitchen and breakfast nook and the family room.

◀Neither upstairs nor down, this broad stair landing quickly became one of the kids' favorite play spots. They're close to the action, but a half-level higher than the adults in the kitchen and breakfast nook.

could just play on it and be in earshot and eye shot. It's the same with the bench in the kitchen. It's a place to relax and sit down in the kitchen, other than at the table. A place to talk to the cook. Play Monopoly. The position of the stair and its landings and openness of stair and landing are very purposeful. Mom said the house should be where kids are comfortable, where they can run around and not have to worry about preserving the house. She wants them to grow up in a place where they can be comfortable."

The main entries for the family are at the rear of the house, from the garage and through a separate back door. Whichever way the kids enter, they go through the mudroom, where low pegs are ready for coats, caps, jackets, and packs. Just past the mudroom is a small pass-through opening to the kitchen. Here Mom can set out snacks or drinks for kids who've just come in from the outside.

Built-In Room for Kids

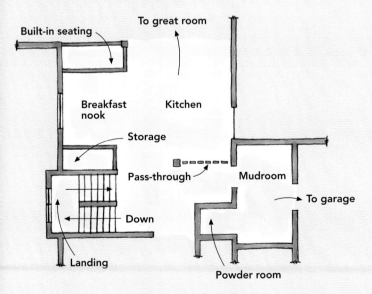

Built-in seating

To great room

Breakfast nook

Kitchen

Storage

Pass-through

Mudroom

To garage

Down

Landing

Powder room

▲While the grownups chat, the kids can draw pictures in a sunny section of the family room. The wall-mounted art center (against the back wall) would be even better if it had hinges so it could fold to form a three-sided playhouse or be closed completely when not in use.

▶Space once wasted as a dining room and porch is used all the time now that it's been turned into a family room. The built-ins have a traditional styling to harmonize with the rest of the room. And the furniture is rugged enough for the kids to use.

Kitchens and Eating Areas

▲ A long, slim counter connects and divides the kitchen and play areas of this open, informal space. The counter and the window seat make good spots for kids to do homework. The built-ins wrap around lockers where children can keep their stuff separate. Even when the kids climb the ladder to the loft, they are within earshot of the kitchen.

The kitchen is the hub of the home. Everyone in the family passes through the kitchen to grab a snack, touch base, or even cook a meal. Kids gravitate here because that's where their parents and the refrigerator are. They stick around to play or do homework.

In the best kitchens, there's a place for kids to do what they do without getting in the way. Small children have an area where they can play without being underfoot, like the little under-counter work area on p. 138. It's also good for older kids to have a spot where they can tackle their homework.

An all-purpose table may be the choice for homework. A small closet off the kitchen can be transformed into a computer station. For little ones, a toy corner or blackboard wall may become a favorite play space.

Broad kitchen islands or peninsulas offer counter space for play or homework. As a bonus, include a lower work surface. For parents, it's a place to work sitting down. For kids, it's a special place where they can help cook. Below the counter, in the section outside the

◀This door from the kitchen to the basement is the family's communications center. The owner of this Chicago home replaced the glazing in a French door with commercial-grade chalkboard on porcelainized steel backing. Now the door holds lists, notes and all the pictures that might otherwise cover the refrigerator.

▲A fold-down stool mounted inside a door brings the microwave or sink within a child's reach. Folding stools like this one are available from numerous manufacturers.

▲The kitchen counter drops down to a table-height section where the kids can do their homework or draw pictures, or the family can grab dinner. Topped with solid surfacing like the other kitchen surfaces, the table blends right in.

kitchen work area, set up storage shelves and cabinets for toys, school supplies, and snacks.

Some parents like under-counter microwaves that their kids can use. Chicago-area designer Jim Garramone created such a place for his daughter. Others believe that all appliances, including microwaves, should be off limits for children. Whatever children use on their own—microwave or kitchen sink—provide a step and adjacent counter space so they can safely reach what they need. ✳

Give Kids a Corner of the Kitchen

Parents can make things easier on themselves if their kids are self-reliant in the kitchen. Give children some cabinet and counter space to call their own, or even a little bit of refrigerator space set aside for them where they can quickly find their favorite snacks. In such cases they're less likely to go to their parents for help.

▲ The end of the kitchen cabinetry facing the family room (in the lower right) becomes a dollhouse. Easy and inexpensive to make, the simple house of shelves gives kids a magical little play corner that's out of the traffic pattern but close to the action.

▶ Nested together to take up little space when not in use, this multipiece kids' station rolls into action at snack or play time. The set features low tables that work as seats, plus higher islands with toy shelves and chalkboard tops. Wood or magnetic strips display kids' artwork without gumming up the wall with tape or making tack holes.

Kitchens Designed with Kids in Mind

For designer Jim Garramone and his family, the kitchen and dining area are just extensions of the living room and family room. Or is it the other way around?

When Garramone remodeled his Chicago-area home, he removed walls and opened up the entire space so that anybody in the kitchen could talk with anybody in the living room, dining room, or family room—and vice versa. And he created the whole open space with an eye to including his daughter in all the family activities.

For instance, the microwave is set into a ventilated pocket just below the counter, a height that's handy for his daughter to make popcorn, but still convenient for the cook. And the family television is just around the corner, inside a built-in cabinet. So when the TV's not on, it's completely hidden. But when the girl wants to watch it, she's near the activity in the kitchen.

Other kids' activities are built into the family area. Garramone divided the living room and dining room space with a small half wall. Within it are shelves that house his daughter's art supplies. So while Mom or Dad is in the kitchen—or watching television—the daughter can color or do homework.

◀Set into a ventilated pocket just below the counter, the microwave oven is handy for kids to make popcorn but still convenient for the adult cooks.

The Kitchen As Family Center

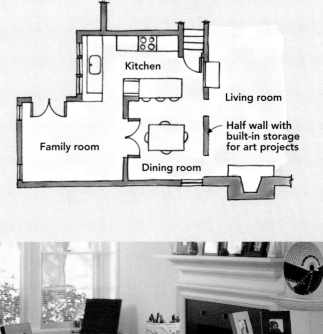

Kitchen

Living room

Family room

Half wall with built-in storage for art projects

Dining room

▲ The end kitchen cabinet facing the family room was built specifically to hold the television and video cassette recorder. The kids can watch the tube near the grownups in the kitchen and the parents can monitor what the kids are watching. The bifold cabinet door does not block views or impede traffic when open.

▲ Disguised to match the other kitchen cabinets and drawers, the three sections of this slim partition between the living and dining areas may be a bit shallow for china but are just right for children's art supplies.

◄Specifically designed for two kids who like to help in the kitchen, this food-preparation area has low, pull-out counters and drawers stocked with cookie cutters, plastic utensils, and snack foods. It's all accessible but out of sight in the a room with a formal patina.

▼Below-counter shelves at this end of the kitchen are reserved for the kids. The cabinet system features two pull-out tables, which have scored laminate tops and segmented backing so they can curve back into the cabinetry like tambour doors.

Some Kitchen Safety Basics

Because the kitchen can be a hazardous place for smaller kids, it's important to remember a few safety precautions. Store matches, knives, and sharp utensils out of reach. Keep hot pots, plates, and drinks far back on the stove or countertop. And unplug appliances when they're not in use so small children won't pull them off by their cords. And when parents are not in the kitchen, the room should be gated to keep out the youngest children.

◄A pocket of open space under the kitchen counter in an out-of-the-way corner is an inspired place for a kids' office. Angled for ease of use, the desk captures light from the patio door and the fixture at the side. The cabinet by the desk holds art supplies.

►The kids have their own kitchen cabinet, strategically positioned between two inviting spots—the table and the window seat. Built-in bins are stocked with art supplies.

Stowing Gear

Boots, coats, gloves, hats, goggles, flippers, cleats, balls, bats, rackets, skates, sticks, helmets, backpacks: An ever-growing collection of clothing and equipment threatens to take over the family home.

Stop this problem at the door by setting up gear zones at the front and the back of the house. All that's needed is a place for the family to stash coats, boots,

◀This pine-walled entryway offers ample storage room for hanging coats, hats, and sports gear. The bench is the right height for young ones to plop down and unburden themselves of packs and boots. Notice the stone-tile floor, which is an appropriately weatherproof surface for a mudroom.

and assorted equipment when entering. Position a bench near the door so kids can sit down to take off their boots. If there are hooks, hat and glove bins, and a boot rack, kids are less likely to dump their outerwear on the floor. If heating runs beneath the boot racks, you have a built-in boot dryer.

A well-planned, easy-to-use mudroom actually teaches kids how to keep things organized. Include storage benches, cubbies, hooks, and shelves designated for different items of clothing and sports paraphernalia. Out-of-season stuff should be stowed elsewhere. If there's not a mudroom, carve one out of an existing space if there's room, like one homeowner in Connecticut did, shown on p. 144.

Each child should have his or her own personal locker or storage area, complete with hooks and shelves within reach. The beauty of adjustable shelves is that they can be raised as the child grows and rearranged to accommodate a variety of gear.

Another option is to line the mudroom with racks. And, ideally, the mudroom should be mud proof. Vinyl flooring, laminate benches, and wire boot racks are good bets. A nearby bathroom is handy for kids to wash up. ✳

▲ ▶ **Utilitarian yet attractive, this bright room** features ample seating and backpack space on deep benches flanking the door. The window seat spans the transitional space between gear area and kitchen. Coats hang in a recess where they are handy but out of the traffic path. The small kids can stand on the bench to hang up their jackets. Cabinets high overhead—even in the soffit space over the window—hold out-of-season gear.

◀When the doors are closed, this wall of broad cabinets extends the sleek, uncluttered look of the adjacent kitchen. The doors hide glorified lockers—one for each kid—outfitted with closet rods, shelves, and two-tiered storage for shoes and boots.

Keep Doormats Inside and Out

If there's no extra room for a dedicated mudroom, here's a tip for at least keeping all the mud the kids track in as close to the front door as possible. Buy two mats, one durable and sturdy to go just outside and a lightweight one for inside. If parents can get their kids to wipe their boots, take them off near the door and leave them there for the next outing, the battle against grime is half over.

◄Packed with storage without seeming stuffed, this mudroom tucks shelves for snow pants between closet rods—the low rod for jackets used daily and the upper one for the rest. The drawer under the bench is deep enough for bulky hats and gloves. Hooks above the bench are a nod to reality: Little kids may hang up their coats on hooks, but forget about hangers.

The Shortest Distance between Two Points

If there's a clear path between an upstairs bath and a downstairs laundry, there's room for a laundry chute, either through the floor or through the wall. In this example, a builder created a durable, snag-free and waterproof laundry chute using heavy-duty 14-in.-dia. PVC pipe.

This type of laundry chute works best if it is designed into the house from the start; that way the two rooms are sure to line up. However, because rooms that contain plumbing are often stacked, chances are good that the chute idea might work anyway. The chute goes between the

floor joists. It's screwed securely to the joists and to blocking that's nailed between the joists.

Be certain to check with the local building inspection department first to make sure your plan meets code requirements.

◄▲Drop wet or dirty clothing down this 14-in.-dia. PVC laundry chute and it falls right into a basket in the laundry room below.

Creating a Mudroom

A family in New England bought a 200-year-old Cape Cod–style house, which was historically all very authentic. That, however, was a problem. The main door to the house opened to what was called the "keeping" room, a long and narrow area with a large central fireplace dominating the space. The problem was that there was nothing dividing the space into useful chunks—no place for the family's two boys to come in, drop their wet boots and packs, and hang up their coats and hats.

The owner could have added a mudroom. But that would've required a building permit, a foundation, and significant cost. Instead, he partitioned off about one-third of the room with a wall made from raised-panel doors bought at the local home center. Four doors—

▲Mudrooms are a modern idea, but they don't have to look modern. This one—with wood paneling, traditional hardware, and hand-crafted closet and bench—fits into a 200-year-old home.

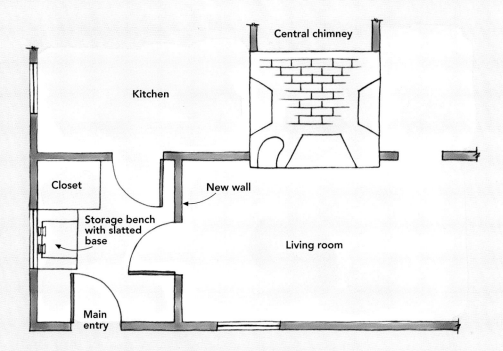

Kitchen

Central chimney

Closet

New wall

Storage bench with slatted base

Living room

Main entry

▲ Built over a hot-air register, the bench has a wood-slat base, which works as a drying box for wet boots and shoes.

three fixed, one operable—box off the mudroom from the main room to the right. A dutch door leads straight ahead into the kitchen. To the left and beneath the window in the new mudroom, he built a bench with operable lid and, beside the box, a floor-to-ceiling coat closet.

The boys can sit on the bench, take off their wet shoes, then drop them inside the bench. That might sound like a good way to keep boots and shoes wet, but the box just happens to be built over a hot-air register. Instead of building a solid bottom on the box, the homeowner built the base out of wooden slats so that air flows through and dries everything nicely for the next day.

Playing Outside

Kids love playing outdoors. Despite the lure of Nintendo, television, the Internet, and air-conditioning, kids still love the classics: tree houses, playhouses, forts, swings, and slides. But like virtually everything nowadays, even outdoor play areas have gotten complicated, elaborate, and often expensive.

The basic ingredients haven't changed, though. Outside as well as inside, a play area needs basic ingredients—a mix of levels, things kids can crawl into or climb over, lookouts, activity zones, and a secret place or two. Even outdoors, kids need a tranquil getaway to be alone and unwind. ✶

▶Colorful, versatile, and extremely fun, a two-towered playset packs a lot into a relatively small footprint. Especially inviting to kids are the lookouts and the tube chute.

◀It's a playhouse, a tower, a bridge—and a set for climbing and sliding. This witty wood castle is a good example of a successful outdoor structure, thanks to these basic elements and all the doors and windows, ins and outs, and ups and downs.

Basic Play Areas

▲Kids love this woodland fort because it's loaded with levels and moving parts: "gun ports" with trapdoors, an observation tower with swinging double-rope ladder, gates with latches, and slide bolts.

Some of the most appealing outdoor play areas are the grow-your-own variety. Kids can't resist a tunnel or arbor covered with vines or branches. A secret enclosure surrounded by shrubs, including perhaps a few topiary animals, is a winner. A steep slope or hill is a great place to carve out a bermed playhouse.

Whether the play spaces are home-grown or home built, kids should be involved in the design process. First, it will be theirs. Second, if it's not theirs they won't use it. Kids as young as three or four and as old as teenagers, have ideas—some of them very specific and elaborate. And many projects can be built in phases, with components prepared in the basement over the winter, for example, and assembled outside come spring. ✳

◀This fort invites high adventure, but it's made from easy-to-find parts. The stockade fencing comes from the local lumberyard; the ladder is a swing set component.

▲Too big to budge, the big boulder in this backyard became the centerpiece of an imagined island, and the rest of the structure was designed and built to take advantage of this natural asset.

◄At one end of the rock, a small platform features a ladder, a bucket pulley, and a slide escape hatch. Beneath is a clubhouse, store front with sliding acrylic plastic window, theater...you name it.

▲No space is wasted in this versatile play space. The platform that bridges the distance to a tree stump has a ramp, slide, peepholes, and "steering station" with wheels and control panel. Underneath is a sandbox.

A Castle and Ship

Architect Steven Bostwick's client knew just what she wanted in her backyard. She even sketched out a detailed plan for him: Put the castle by the big tree at the stream bank and run a suspension bridge across to a raised platform with a lookout point. Her concept was very specific, very detailed—benches go here, fireman's pole there, cargo net ladder off to the side. The elementary school student clearly knew her own mind.

Bostwick, who spends much of his time designing and building play structures, always sits down with his clients to ferret out what's on their wish list. In this case, eight-year-old Rachel was the primary spokesperson, since her brothers were only five and one.

Using Rachel's sketch as a launching point, Bostwick designed a structure that evokes a castle but could also be whatever else the kids imagine. He built the components in his shop using pressure-treated lumber that he hand-picked and planed. Bostwick always recommends that a water-repellent sealer be applied.

Tucked against a knoll to command views of approaching enemies, the castle features a turret-like lookout tower with

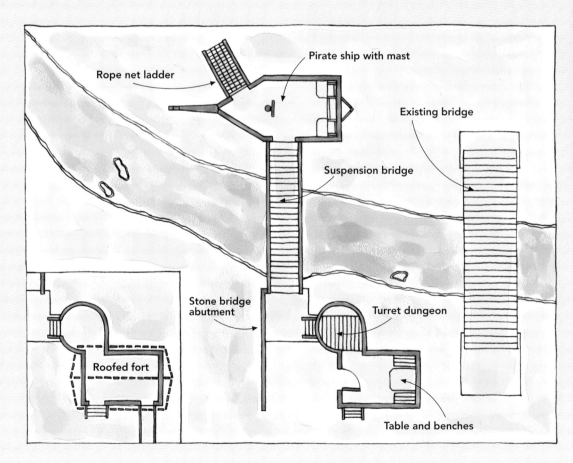

Rope net ladder

Pirate ship with mast

Existing bridge

Suspension bridge

Stone bridge abutment

Turret dungeon

Roofed fort

Table and benches

This dynamic structure has many different levels; both closed and open spaces; and several ways to get in, out, up, and down.

▼Kids love the intrigue and adventure of the tower, dungeon, and bridge. Adults appreciate the craftsmanship and beauty of the structure and the way it's integrated into the landscape.

ladder and slide. The room below with the little door and the built-in table can be a dungeon or clubhouse. A suspension bridge stretches from a stone abutment and leads to a stylized pirate ship fitted with mast and helm. The fireman's pole, cargo net ladder, and benches are all there, just as Rachel requested. She also wanted a good, old-fashioned tire swing. It's there, too, hanging from a high branch on a nearby tree.

Playhouses

◀ If there's no tree, it's not a problem. This post-mounted lodge has all the best features of a tree house, including rope ladder, trapdoor, and hook-and-pulley for hoisting supplies. A rear wall encloses the space, but parents can keep an eye on things from the front. The homeowner pre-assembled and notched sections of the structure so they dropped into place with ease.

I nside the house and most other places kids go, they're little fish in a big pond. Counters are tall, windows are high, furniture is big, ceilings stratospheric. Kids are bound to feel puny, sometimes overwhelmed, perhaps unimportant. But one foot inside the playhouse door and they are transformed.

▲ This sod-roofed house has redwood bark walls that are weather resistant and a waterproof membrane that keeps the roof from leaking. Rainwater drains into a sprinkling can over the flower box. A little embedded sprinkler system will keep the grass green.

Great playhouses run the gamut from rustic huts to gingerbread beauties to miniature renditions of real houses. Kids love having a little house decked out with fanciful trim and bright colors. Then again, they'll probably have just as much fun with a simple, unpainted box. The key is the word *little*. Cut down the scale of the playhouse so it's just right for kids and unquestionably too small for adults. Make it their size and you make it theirs. ✳

Give Kids Varied Outdoor Options

The best outdoor structures give children a variety of options for play and make-believe. They blend with the site and give kids the opportunity to challenge themselves, experiment, and take a few risks. A good play space also gives kids a place to hide—to get away from other children or adults and to escape into their own imaginations.

▲ Complete with white picket fence and four furnished rooms, this mini-house works great for kids who like to play house. The owner made the walls in his basement one winter, then put them up when the snow melted.

Carefully Plan where to Put Outdoor Structures

Before buying a playhouse—whether prefabricated or prebuilt—get the dimensions of the playhouse and take a survey of your backyard to decide the best location for it. If you decide to put it under a tree, make sure the playhouse isn't so tall that it won't fit neatly beneath the limbs. And choose a spot that can be viewed from the back porch or a rear window of the house so you can keep an eye on the kids.

▲The owner built the breakfast table and bench seats and cut the store-bought coffee table down to size to complement the child-size scale of this playhouse.

▶From the windows to the trim, everything about this carefully designed and built playhouse is accurate in scale and function. It really is a miniature house just for kids.

Outdoor Building Materials

The materials in a playhouse, fort, or tree house should be high on durability and low on maintenance.

For wood, choose straight, uniform pieces with as few knots as possible. Durable, rot-resistant exterior woods such as redwood, cedar, and mahogany are best for outdoor structures. Pressure-treated lumber, however, is much less expensive. It's usually made from southern yellow pine, Douglas fir, or spruce. It's highly rot resistant, which makes it ideal for posts that come in contact with the ground and for surfaces that will bear the brunt of weather. Although pressure-treated wood has been subject to controversy, it's basically a safe material for outdoor use. One caution, however: Once a structure is built with pressure-treated lumber, safely dispose of waste.

Synthetic lumber is another option. It's considerably more expensive than conventional lumber but extremely long lasting. Try Trex wood, Perma-Wood, or ChoiceDek. Though recycled from either plastic or plastic and wood fibers, these products look a lot like real lumber and cut just the same way. Use them for handrails, tabletops, or floors, if well supported from underneath.

Elements of Outdoor Play

The most interesting outdoor structures mix levels, shapes, sizes, and equipment in lively combination. Kids climb a ladder to a playhouse, for instance, then shoot out the slide at the back or cross a bridge to a lookout post, slide down a fireman's pole, slip into the hideaway below the lookout, crawl through a tunnel, and send up a message in a bucket and with a pulley.

Level ground is fine for an integrated play structure, but irregular terrain adds to the excitement. Bumps, gentle slopes, and gullies are great launching points for bridges, ladders, and ground slides. Steeper hillsides invite cantilevered structures, with sandboxes, playhouses, or tire swings underneath. Boulders and tree stumps make dramatic perches for boardwalks and lookouts.

At a minimum, a play structure should feature swings, a slide, and a small enclosure or playhouse type of space. But many extras and options exist to complement these basics. Adding two or three enclosed areas at different points and levels in the structure—some sprouting from decks and others tucked into shady recesses—creates interest. Don't forget to incorporate monkey bars, rope ladders, fireman's poles, zip lines, and lots of entrances and exits, some of them "secret" ones with trapdoors.

Channel a ribbon of "tunnels"—tubing pierced with window holes—along the ground or just above it. Run a balance bar across the grass, maybe in a circle or figure eight. Build a small climbing wall. Link the play structure to a tree house or crow's nest via a ladder, spiral ramp, or winding stairs.

The play structure shown above is tempting yet safe for little kids. This bright assembly contains the basics and some extras: see-through railings and nonslippery decking made of a wood and plastic composite, a bucket pulley, "telephones" wired with garden hoses (you can't see them in the photo), and a ripple slide. While the kids swing at one wing of the structure, their parents can relax in the bench swing at the other end.

▲Alluring yet safe for little children, this bright ensemble has high, see-through railings and nonslippery decking made of a wood and plastic composite. Details include a bucket pulley, "telephones" wired with garden hoses (not shown), and a rippled slide. And parents can watch from the swing at the other end.

If there's a storage shed in the backyard, cap it off with a playhouse. The kids who live here have picnics and club meetings in this breezy summer retreat, which sits atop a 10-ft. by 10-ft. shed. A sturdy ladder hooks into place but can be rolled aside to make way for lawn work.

This little playhouse on stilts with its Alice-in-Wonderland door is equipped with a built-in activity table and enough room to hold three sleeping bags for overnights. The enclosed structure also forms a roof over the sandbox. Safe, operable windows capture breezes so the bright, skylighted space doesn't get stuffy. Adults enjoy the playhouse because its white columns, fine woods, and craftsman details make it a sophisticated landscape asset.

◄**Order extra roofing and** siding for a remodeling or new house project, and use the surplus to build a miniature house in the backyard. Even if fancy decorative trim is added, it will cost less thanks to the discount on volume purchase. This older playhouse, with custom-crafted windows and doors, is an inspiration for such a project. Unique touches include awning, doorbell, vintage doorknob, and classic curtains.

►**It's small, odd-shaped, and three levels—** in other words, this playhouse is perfect for kids' adventures. The first floor has a kid-size door, shuttered windows, door knocker, and mail slot. Upstairs is a balcony and a tiny attic space, accessible only to the smallest ones.

Details Make Playhouses Come Alive

For parents who have a working knowledge of carpentry and construction, crafting a playhouse can be a fun and rewarding project. Depending on the skill level, a parent can make the playhouse as simple or as complex as desired. Just remember that detailing is what makes a playhouse come alive. That includes door, windows, siding, trim, roofing, and porch or railings. Though the details cost the most and require the most time to build or install, without them the playhouse is just a box.

▲Planks and paint can add up to an imaginative playhouse. This artistic structure is loaded with clever touches that appeal to kids: keyhole windows, a mail slot, and doors and shutters that open and close.

▼A triangle of trees supports this good-looking, three-cornered structure. Kids can climb up one of the ladders to the deck or sidle over from the monkey bars and through the pagoda windows. They have a choice of swings, too—the set attached to the cross bar or the all-weather tire model under the deck.

Consider a Few Safety Precautions

Run through a safety checklist to make sure your kid's playsets don't invite mishaps. Wood corners should be rounded smooth. Structures higher than 2½ ft. need guard rails. Chains should be covered with plastic or rubber tubing to avoid pinches. And to prevent fall injuries don't cover the ground around playsets with hard material; instead, use wood mulch or fine sand.

Tree Houses

Nothing beats a good tree house. Whether it's scabbed together with discarded planking or an architect-designed palace, kids want a perch in the trees. An old, large tree is sort of the ideal site for a tree house. Another great tree-house site is a cluster of trees with attached aerial walkways that weave through the backyard. Even if the trees don't provide the actual structural support, the platform can be tucked against the trees while wood posts resting on concrete footings do the work.

Getting into the tree house should be an adventure in itself. Kids might use a plank ladder or stairway to carry up supplies. Other times they'll take a swashbuckling approach, reaching up a knotted rope, a dangling rope ladder, a climbing wall, or a trail of slats up a tree trunk. Just for fun, include one or two quick-exit routes from the tree house, such as a slide or a fireman's pole reached through a small portal. Zip lines are great. And trapdoors add to the intrigue, although they carry the

▲ A tree-studded lot may be tight on ground-level play space, but it's perfect for a "trees" house. This one stretches all the way to a lookout at the edge of the woods. Next summer's project might be to add a rope ladder or build an upper level platform on the tree that pokes through the main deck.

increased risk of pinched fingers and bumped heads. To send notes or toys or sandwiches up to the tree house, children still love the classic rope, bucket, and pulley.

Even the simplest platform tree house can have a sheltered corner with roof and walls, a small enclosure where kids can set up a club or go to read, play games, or have sleepovers. On the following pages are outstanding tree houses that do all those things—some spectacular and elaborate, others simple and built with found materials. ✳

▼Tucked between trees, this lean-to is a pocket of adventure. From the deck, kids can shimmy up trunks and swing from overhanging limbs. The rope rail adds to the Tarzan aura, but still to come is crosshatching with a web of rope between railings for safety.

An Elegant Tree House

Builder Josh Baker of BOWA Builders in Arlington, Virginia, and architect Michael Medick of Columbia, Maryland, were used to building houses rooted to the ground, so the commission for an elaborate tree house was something new and challenging.

"I designed a tree house for my own kids, but not to this level of design and scale," Medick said. "It won a local design award and some people saw that in the paper and called us. We went out as a team, the builder and I, and did the design."

The first thing Medick and Baker did was to call in an arborist to ensure that the large old dogwood wouldn't be harmed in the process. Building around a growing tree presents a number of challenges, not the least of which is ensuring that the tree can continue to grow and flex in the wind without damaging itself or the tree house. In this tree house, the design called for one large branch to actually penetrate the roof of the house through a porch-like overhang.

"We cut sufficient room in the roof for the tree to grow and fabricated a gasket around it so the tree can breathe," Medick said. In their favor was the age of the tree, said Baker. "We minimized physical attachments. And we used gaskets improvised by guys in the field and by some roofers. The gasket is some sort of rubber. But that's a mature dogwood tree. It's not an oak tree that has a lot of growth potential, so it's not going to grow that much more."

▶ Tree houses are the most attractive to children when they're scaled to the size of kids. Here, the dormers, windows, and ceiling height are all in proportion to the children who enjoy this elegant tree house.

A Tree House Estate

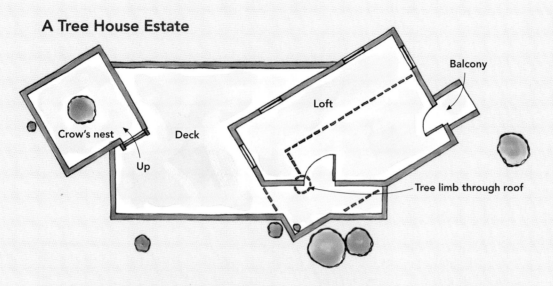

For continued stability, Medick and Baker poured a series of concrete footings in the ground to support posts for the structure. Although the tree house is bolted to the tree (actually two trees, counting the one with the crow's nest), the posts carry much of the load. "The tree house is supported by posts on the ground as opposed to just the tree itself," Medick said. "We tried to tuck those back as far as possible, to give appearance of floating in space."

It might not be clear from the photos, but the tree house is definitely scaled to a child's size, which Medick said is im-

portant to remember during design. "The idea was to have deck space for a play area for the kids. And to have the house itself. It's on an Alice-in-Wonderland scale. Looking at the door to the tree house, if an adult was standing at the door, his or her head would be in the rafters. That's how small it is. So it's really kid size.

▶Inside the tree house it's shady and cool, though ample windows, both downstairs and up, provide great views through the treetops and let in filtered light.

▲▼Some trees like this one are made for tree houses. A ladder up to the lofty platform hugs a cluster of trunks. A trapdoor covers the entry opening in the floor. Although this is a very basic tree structure, the kids like it so much they marked it with their names and handprints.

Choosing the Right Tree

The best tree houses are in the best trees. If choices abound, go for an older tree that offers a good, fairly low spot between a few thick limbs. The higher the tree house, the greater the chance wind will damage it. The thicker the limbs, the stronger, so it's better to anchor the tree house to a few big limbs than to a number of smaller ones. And the fewer the limbs required to support the tree house, the simpler the job becomes.

▲ ▶ This elaborate and elegant tree house includes a second story with dormer; loft accessed by a series of ladders; and across the rope bridge to a lookout tower. The tree house has a fireman's pole escape and rope ladder to a secret trapdoor. The loft sleeps three.

A Scavenged Tree House

Interesting ideas grow on trees at Dave Albert's place. Take this work-in-progress. After helping a friend dismantle an old summer cabin, Albert brought some of the materials back to his rural property outside Watsonville, California.

He leaned the cabin staircase against a large old eucalyptus tree, and suddenly got an idea. Add a platform on top and call it a tree house.

The platform went up—followed by a number of other things. The two-story tree house now has a slide, a second-floor balcony, and two beds used often for overnights. Albert wired the place so the kids have light at night—or can watch television. A sturdy, 1½-in.-thick rope swing hangs from a branch 80 ft. high. Recent additions include double zip lines the kids can board from the tree house deck. They ride the 160-ft. lines to and from the tree house.

For Albert and his sons, part of the fun of creating the evolving tree house project has been scavenging building materials for

◀The rope swing tied high up in the tree of this California tree house is strong enough to hold several kids at once. The father periodically checks it, however, for wear and tear.

◀A tree house is great, and a slide is great. But combine the two, and it's an unbeatable combination for children.

▼Inside the tree house, kids can hang from overhead grips attached to the bottom of the top bunk. So, if they fall, they land on the mattress below.

it. The stairs and front door come from the old cabin. The light fixtures are secondhand too. The inside walls of the house are panels from machinery packing crates. Those acrylic plastic sliding windows? Leftover machine guards.

The kids, now preteens, have helped build the tree house since the start, taking bigger roles as they've gotten older. Now the older boy is looking to build his own fort at the top of a hill on the property. Albert's thinking of connecting the two play structures with zip lines. The kids "have lots of adventures planned out," he says. And they've got a dad who is willing to make those adventures possible.

Resources

Books and Pamphlets

Bunting, Eve. *Sunflower House.* New York: Harcourt Brace, 1996. A picture book for young children showing how to create a sunflower playhouse.

Dannenmaier, Molly. *A Child's Garden.* New York: Simon & Schuster, 1998. Contains designs for children's outdoor spaces that incorporate nature.

Susanka, Sarah, with Kira Obolensky. *The Not So Big House.* Newtown, Conn.: The Taunton Press, 1998. Contains ideas for the design of family houses that use space well and answer the needs of kids and adults.

Tolpin, Jim, with Mary Lathrop. *The New Family Home.* Newtown, Conn.: The Taunton Press, 2000. Covers a variety of houses created with families in mind.

Magazines

Most home decorating, lifestyle, and parenting magazines run occasional articles on design of kids' spaces. Best bets are *Better Homes and Gardens, Child, House Beautiful, Parents Magazine, Southern Living,* and *Sunset.* Other magazines to check are *Country Living, Family Circle, Good Housekeeping, Ladies' Home Journal, Parenting, Today's Homeowner,* and *Woman's Day.*

For articles that go further, telling how to build the featured kids' structures, *Fine Homebuilding* is great. Also worth checking: *Family Handyman, Popular Mechanics,* and *Workbench.*

Web Sites

www.cpsc.gov
U.S. Consumer Product Safety Commission site features bulletins on product safety and guidelines on the design of safe spaces. Bulletins appear on the site; go to "Consumer," then "Publications."

www.drtoy.com
Covers play environments, and has links to many related sites. Dr. Toy is Stevanne Auerbach, Ph.D., director of the Institute for Childhood Resources in San Francisco and author of the syndicated "Dr. Toy" newspaper column. Auerbach is author of *Dr. Toy's Smart Play* (St. Martin's Griffin, 1998).

www.msro.com/ro/
Ro Logrippo's site focuses on design of children's spaces. Logrippo owns Living & Learning Environments in Burlingame, California. Her books include *In My World* (John Wiley & Sons, 1995) and *In My Room* (Fawcett/Columbine, 1989).

www.safebaby.net
Includes extensive safety guidelines for kids' spaces. The site belongs to Barbara Sklar, R.N., a specialist in safe environments for infants and toddlers.

Professional Organizations

American Institute of Architects, 1735 New York Avenue NW, Washington, DC 20006
Many architects are members of AIA. The Web site will help you find AIA architects who do residential work in your area (www.aiaaccess.com).

American Society of Interior Designers, 608 Massachusetts Avenue NE, Washington, DC 20002
For names of ASID members in your town, call the referral service at 800-775-2743 or go to the Web site (www.interiors.org).

Decorating Den Interiors, 19100 Montgomery Village Avenue, #200, Montgomery Village, MD 20886
To get names of Decorating Den designers in your area, call 800-DEC-DENS or visit the Web site (www.decoratingden.com).

National Association of Home Builders, 1201 Fifteenth Street NW, Washington, DC 20005
Membership includes home builders and remodelers. Remodeler members who complete a professional certification program have the Certified Graduate Remodelor (CGR) designation. The Web site features consumer pages on planning a remodeling project and choosing a contractor (www.nahb.com).

National Association of the Remodeling Industry, 4900 Seminary Road, #3210, Alexandria, VA 22311
Members include general remodelers and specialty contractors. Members who complete a certification program earn Certified Remodeler (CR) credentials. The Web site provides consumer information on designing a remodeling project and selecting a remodeler (www.remodeltoday.com).

National Kitchen & Bath Association, 687 Willow Grove Street, Hackettstown, NJ 07840
Organization of kitchen and bath design specialists, including those who have earned Certified Kitchen Designer (CKD) and Certified Bath Designer (CBD) designation. The Web site displays award-winning projects, offers remodeling tips, and lists design guidelines for safe kitchens (www.nkba.com).

p. 61: (left) Photo © Jessie Walker, Design: Mastro & Skylar Architects, Chicago, Ill.; (right) Photos © Kent Van Slyke, Design © Solia Hermes, Seattle, Wash.

pp. 62–63: Photos by Charles Miller, courtesy *Fine Homebuilding* magazine, © The Taunton Press, Inc., Design: Ross Chapin Architects, Langley, Wash.

pp. 64–65: Photos © David Duncan Livingston, Design: Greg Collins, Modesto, Calif.

p. 66: Photos © Philip Beaurline, Design: MGD Design/Build, Kensington, Md.

p. 67: Photos © Philip Beaurline, Design: Andy Gilbert, Hopkins & Porter Construction, Potomac, Md.

pp. 68–69: Photos © Kerry Hayes, Design: D'Arcy Dunal Architect, Toronto, Ontario, Canada.

p. 70: Photo © Tim Street-Porter.

p. 71: Photo © Carolyn L. Bates.

p. 72: (top) Photo © Tim Street-Porter; (bottom) Photo © Randy O'Rourke, Design: Lasley Construction and Brahaney Architecture Associates, Rocky Hill, N.J.

p. 73: Photo © Jessie Walker.

p. 74: (top) Photos © Brian Vanden Brink, Design: Stephen Vlachos, CBD, CKD, Atlantic Kitchen Center, Portland, Maine; (bottom) Photo © Eric Roth/Henderson Studio.

p. 75: Photo courtesy Kohler Company, Design: Cheryl Janz, ASID, Oak Brook, Ill.

p. 76: Photo © Barry Halkin, Design: CH Designs, Philadelphia, Pa., Architect: Richard M. Cole & Associates, Philadelphia, Pa.

p. 77: Photos © Randy O'Rourke, Design: Dan Lenner, CKD, CBD, Morris Black Kitchens & Baths, Lehigh Valley, Pa.

p. 78: Photo © David Duncan Livingston.

p. 79: Photo © Thomas Lawrence, Lawrence Architecture.

p. 80: Photos courtesy California Closets.

p. 81: (top) Photo © Andrew Bordwin; (bottom) Photo © David Duncan Livingston.

p. 82: Photos © Jessie Walker.

p. 83: Photo © Tim Ebert, Design: Charm & Whimsy, New York, N.Y.

p. 84: (top) Photo © Tim Street-Porter; (bottom) Photo © Andrew Bordwin.

p. 85: Photo © David Duncan Livingston.

p. 86: Photo © Norman McGrath/Esto Photographics.

p. 87: (right) Photo by Charles Miller, courtesy *Fine Homebuilding* magazine, © The Taunton Press, Inc., Design: Jean Steinbrecher, AIA, Langley, Wash.

pp. 88–89: Photos © Christian Korab, Design: Michaela Mahady, AIA, and Wayne Branum, SALA Architects, Inc., Stillwater, Minn.

pp. 90–91: Photos © Mary Ludington, Design: SALA Architects, Inc., Minneapolis, Minn.

pp. 92–93: Photos © David Duncan Livingston, Design: SawHorse, Inc., Atlanta, Ga.

p. 94: (left) Photo © Peter Paige.

pp. 94–95: (top) Photo © Andrew Bordwin.

p. 95: (right) Photo © Andrew Bordwin.

p. 96: (top) Photo © David Duncan Livingston; (bottom) Photo © Steve Vierra Photography.

p. 97: Photo © Phillip H. Ennis Photography.

p. 98: Photos © Tom Kessler, Kessler Photography, Design: Lori Krejci, AIA, Avant Architects, Inc., Omaha, Nebr.

p. 99: (top) Photo © Tom Kessler, Kessler Photography, Design: Lori Krejci, AIA, Avant Architects, Inc., Omaha, Nebr.; (bottom) Photo © Barry Halkin, Design: Metcalfe + Tsirantonakis Associates, Philadelphia, Pa.

p. 100: Photos © Michael Shemchuk, Design: Art/Decor, Berkeley, Calif.

p. 101: Photos © David Duncan Livingston, Design: Phil Harrison, AIA, Atlanta, Ga.

pp. 102–103: Photos © David Duncan Livingston, Design: SawHorse, Inc., Atlanta, Ga.

p. 104: Photos © Brian Vanden Brink, Design: Stephen Foote, FAIA, Perry Dean Rogers & Partners, Architects, Boston, Mass.

p. 105: Photo © David Duncan Livingston, Design: Ross Chapin Architects, Langley, Wash.

p. 106: (top) Photo by Charles Miller, courtesy *Fine Homebuilding* magazine, © The Taunton Press, Inc., Design: Jean Steinbrecher, AIA, Langley, Wash.; (bottom) Photo © Brian Vanden Brink.

p. 107: Photo © Dale Mulfinger, Design: Dale Mulfinger, SALA Architects, Inc., Minneapolis, Minn.

p. 108: Photo © Tim Ebert, Design: Charm & Whimsy, New York, N.Y.

p. 109: Photos © Bradley Olman, Design: Terri Ervin, Decorating Den Interiors, Dacula, Ga.

p. 110: (top) Photo © Randy O'Rourke, Design: Chuck Green, Four Corners Construction, Ashland, Mass.; (bottom) Photo © Pete Hecht/Mark Lisk Studio, Design: Strite Design + Remodel, Boise, Idaho.

p. 111: Photo © Mary Ludington, Design: Hendrickson.

p. 112: Photo © Dave Adams, Design: Molly Korb, CKD, CBD, MK Designs, Newcastle, Calif.

p. 113: Photos © Andrew Bordwin.

p. 114: Photo © Cheryl Ungar, Design: Doug Walter, Denver, Colo.

p. 115: (top) Photo © Mark Lohman Photography; (bottom) Photo by David Duncan Livingston, © The Taunton Press, Inc., Design: Katherine Cartrette, SALA Architects, Inc., Stillwater, Minn.

p. 116: Photos © Mark Lohman Photography.

p. 117: Photo © David Duncan Livingston, Design: Jennifer Randall Associates, Seattle, Wash.

p. 118: (top) Photo © Mary Ludington, Design: SALA Architects, Inc., Minneapolis, Minn.; (bottom) Photo © Kerry Hayes, Design: D'Arcy Dunal Architect, Toronto, Ontario, Canada.

p. 119: Photos © Del Brown, Design: Bob Bouril, Bouril Design Studio, Madison, Wis.

p. 120: Photos © David Duncan Livingston.

p. 121: (top) Photo © Eric Roth/Henderson Studio; (bottom) Photo © Tria Giovan.

p. 122: Photo by David Duncan Livingston, © The Taunton Press, Inc., Design: Brian Cearnal, Santa Barbara, Calif.

p. 123: (right) Photo © Carolyn L. Bates.

p. 124: Photo © Darris Harris, Design: Morgante-Wilson Architects, Chicago, Ill.

p. 125: Photo by David Duncan Livingston, © The Taunton Press, Inc., Design: Andy Neumann, Architect, Carpenteria, Calif.

p. 126: Photo © Darris Harris, Design: Morgante-Wilson Architects, Chicago, Ill.

p. 127: Photos © Randy O'Rourke.

p. 128: Photo © Philip Beaurline, Design: Laurent Lafleur, Columbia, Md.

pp. 130–131: Photos by David Duncan Livingston, © The Taunton Press, Inc., Design: Michaela Mahady, AIA, SALA Architects, Inc., Stillwater, Minn.

p. 132: (top) Photo © Tim Street-Porter; (bottom) Photo © Philip Beaurline, Design: MGD Design-Build, Kensington, Md.

p. 133: Photo © David Duncan Livingston.

p. 134: (left) Photo courtesy General Electric; (top right) Photo by Charles Miller, courtesy *Fine Homebuilding* magazine, © The Taunton Press, Inc., Design: Jim Garramone, Garramone Design, Evanston, Ill.; (bottom right) Photo © Carolyn L. Bates.

p. 135: (top) Photo © Pete Hecht/Mark Lisk Studio, Design: Stronghold Construction, Boise, Idaho; (bottom) Photo © Phillip H. Ennis Photography.

pp. 136–137: Photos © Darris Harris, Design: Jim Garramone, Garramone Design, Evanston, Ill.

p. 138: (top) Photo © Craig Burleigh, Design: Marilyn A. Woods, CKD, ASID Allied Member, Mountain View, Calif.; (bottom) Photo © David Duncan Livingston, Design: Marcia Miller, ASID, and Steven Stein, ASID, Miller/Stein, Menlo Park, Calif.

p. 139: (top) Photo by Charles Miller, courtesy *Fine Homebuilding* magazine, © The Taunton Press, Inc., Design: Ann Finnerty, Boston, Mass.; (bottom) Photo © Darris Harris, Design: Morgante-Wilson Architects, Chicago, Ill.

p. 140: Photo © Eric Roth/Henderson Studio.

p. 141: Photos © Darris Harris, Design: Morgante-Wilson Architects, Chicago, Ill.

p. 142: Photos © David Leale, Design: Stephanie Witt, CKD, Kitchens by Stephanie, Grand Rapids, Mich.

p. 143: (top) Photo © Darris Harris, Design: Morgante-Wilson Architects, Chicago, Ill.; (bottom left and right) Photos by Andy Engel, courtesy *Fine Homebuilding* magazine, © The Taunton Press, Inc., Design: Byron Papa, Durham, N.C.

pp. 144–145: Photos © Randy O'Rourke.

p. 146: Photo © Teena Albert, Design: Barbara Butler, Artist-Builder, San Francisco, Calif.

p. 147: (right) Photo by Guy Reynolds, courtesy *Fine Homebuilding* magazine, © The Taunton Press, Inc., Design: Daniel B. Johnson, Noblesville, Ind.

p. 148: Photos © Randy O'Rourke, Design: Patricia F. Eastman, Freehold, N.J.

p. 149: Photos © Randy O'Rourke, Design: KidSpace Inc., Canton Center, Conn.

p. 151: Photos © Steven J. Bostwick, Design: Steven J. Bostwick Architect, Wyoming, Ohio.

p. 152: Photo © Will Hubbell, Design: Will Hubbell, Rochester, N.Y.

p. 153: Photo © John Larson, Design: John Larson, Jarvis Architects, Oakland, Calif.

pp. 154–155: Photos © Jeff Burns, Design: Jeff Burns, Scituate, Mass.

p. 156: Photo © Rob Karosis, Design: David Gingrich, Gilford, N.H.

p. 157: (top left) Photo © Darris Harris, Design: Morgante-Wilson Architects, Chicago, Ill.; (top right and bottom) Photos © Randy O'Rourke, Design: Robert A. Weiss, Glenwood Landing, N.Y.

p. 158: (top) Photo © Brian Vanden Brink; (bottom) Photo © Teena Albert, Design: Barbara Butler, Artist-Builder, San Francisco, Calif.

p. 159: (top) Photo © Teena Albert, Design: Barbara Butler, Artist-Builder, San Francisco, Calif.; (bottom) Photo © Kimberley Fiterman, Design: Kimberley Fiterman, ASID, Funtastic Interiors, New York, N.Y.

pp. 160–161: Photos © Martin Webster, Design: Martin Webster Landscape Design & Construction, Brattleboro, Vt.

pp. 162–163: Photos © John Cleave, Design: Michael K. Medick, Baltimore, Md., Builder: BOWA Builders, McLean, Va.

p. 164: Photos © David Leale.

p. 165: Photos © Steven J. Bostwick, Design: Steven J. Bostwick Architect, Wyoming, Ohio.

pp. 166–167: Photos © Mary Altier, Design: Dave Albert, Watsonville, Calif.